ADVANCE PRAISE FOR

One Thought Away

"Kerry is a leader that is driven to help women do whatever it takes to have the life of their dreams. She leads by inspired storytelling, her vulnerability, and willingness to stay the student herself. This is a must read for every woman ready to uplevel her life."

JJ Virgin, Celebrity Nutrition and Fitness Expert
and four-time NY Times Bestselling Author

"A good spiritual kick in the rear! One I'll read again. I think if you are self-employed, like I am, this is a must read!"

David M. Corbin, four-time Wall Street Journal
and USAToday Bestselling Author

"After reading this book, you can literally jump into taking immediate action. All of the nuggets and insight make this more than a read, it's like a 'dream life' workbook."

Dr. Mariza Snyder, Author of National Bestselling book,
The Essential Oils Hormone Solution

"If you are ready to understand how great you really are, ready to lay down limiting beliefs and self-doubts, One Thought Away will take you there! Each chapter is designed to supercharge you with energy, insight, and possibility, as you create the most powerful and best version of yourself."

Arielle Ford, Author of *Love Thief*

"Unleash the power of your journey by reframing your thoughts. Transform what once held you back into opportunities for growth, one thought at a time."

Taylor Leigh Cannizzaro,
Chief Relationship Officer at Plastic Bank

"One Thought Away is one of the simplest, yet most effective, approaches for how you can manage your beliefs and actions to create your dream life. You want that from someone who has known and lived every facet they deliver. I've known Kerry through the years and can personally attest to how Kerry is that inspiring real deal who LIVES these concepts, has created incredible results out of seemingly impossible circumstances, and helps heart-driven women do the same. She is mission-driven to change women's lives beyond what they ever thought possible. So, YOUR dream life is literally one action step away—which is, getting "One Thought Away" and reading it NOW!"

Lynn Rose, Media Entrepreneur, CEO, WOWUNOW

KERRY TEPEDINO, HHP, CCN, CST

One Thought Away

YOU ARE ONE THOUGHT
AWAY FROM HAVING YOUR
DREAM LIFE, OR NOT

One Thought Away

Kerry Tepedino

Copyright © 2023

ISBN: 979-8-9881998-0-9

Garlic Bulb Enterprise, Inc.

315 S Coast Hwy 101

Encinitas, CA 92024

Printed in the United States of America

Table of Contents

Introduction

How Embodying One Thought Away
Can Change Your Life

*Y*ou're one thought away from having an incredible life ... or not.

"This is no way to live," I cried. "It's also not the way I want to die. What am I doing to myself?"

In retrospect, the better question was, "Why am I doing this to myself?" because I knew exactly what it was that I was doing. And I was angry and upset with myself for doing it.

"Kerry, I can't believe you let this happen *again!* Binging and purging are killing you, and you're smarter than that!"

The words I told myself were true, but I had no idea how to break the cycle.

That night had been building up for years. I'd never felt like I was good enough, and as a person who needed to feel like I was in control, I turned to eating to give me a quick hit of relief. It gave me a rush of dopamine.

I thought I could control my eating, but it obviously backfired. I didn't have the coping skills to deal with my feelings, especially the lows of a normal life. I used food as a vice to check out, numb out and escape.

In hindsight, that night was a blessing in my life. It was a turning point ... but I didn't know it at the time. After returning from a two-year stint in the Peace Corps, I was working as a graphic designer for a startup software company in Southern California. I had a deadline to meet on a major project the next day. I was scared of not meeting expectations and nervous about what my boss and peers would think of me and my work, so I tried to calm my stress levels by eating.

It was dark, and I was driving home from work, hands on the wheel, saying to myself, "Don't stop at the store, Kerry. Don't stop at the store." I didn't need groceries.

But where did I find myself when I pulled into my neighborhood? At the store, even though I knew better.

Going into the store, I repeated to myself, "This time, it's going to be different."

I grabbed a shopping cart, and as I walked up and down the aisles, I filled my cart with all of my favorite comfort foods. Of course, all the while I told myself that the groceries would last a couple weeks, like they would for any "normal" person.

Paying for the groceries, I continued to repeatedly tell myself that things would be different this time. Once home, I was unpacking the bags and putting the food away, and my hand found the peanut butter jar. After unscrewing the familiar blue lid, I peeled back the silver foil and grabbed a spoon. I convinced myself that I was going to take just one bite.

Yeah, right. I was hungry. After all, I hadn't eaten all day.

One spoonful turned into two, two into three, and before I knew it, my spoon hit the bottom of the jar, and my heart broke.

Once again, I'd betrayed myself.

I quickly made my way down the hall to the bathroom, where my now too common cycle repeated itself of trying to purge out the food. I caught a glimpse of myself in the bathroom mirror and saw shame and loathing in my eyes, looking back at me.

"What is wrong with me? What can't I just get this right?"

But that night was different than all the rest.

After turning on myself with purging, I crumbled onto the cold, small square white tiles that covered the floor. There was an acidic taste in my mouth, and I was covered with a light film of sweat. My heart was racing so fast and hard that it scared me.

"Kerry, you're killing yourself!"

I knew better and couldn't claim ignorance as an excuse. The mother of a dear friend passed away from an eating disorder, because her organs failed, so I knew what could happen to me if I persisted in this self-abuse.

It was the first time I *REALLY* realized that it could happen to me, too. It stopped me in my tracks.

"Kerry, if you don't turn this around, you are going to die."

My Defining Moment

I was in a defining moment … either find a way to get myself up off that bathroom floor and turn my life around, or I'd slowly kill myself if I continued this destructive bulimic behavior. I was terrified that I wouldn't get the opportunity to live a full life, and I decided I had something to live for.

I wanted to live!

Today, I look back on that moment, and I am in shock and awe that I found my way out of that living hell. I have since dropped to my knees in massive gratitude for that moment, because it changed the trajectory of my life.

That night, I gained awareness that brought me to a place where I can share my story and help others who are experiencing similar anguish.

Their pain might not look exactly the way mine did, but they have their own version of it. It could be eating away at their soul right now.

Maybe it is eating away at your soul, too.

What if it's one reason you are reading this book? Perhaps you manifested this book finding you, the information and tools it's going to supply you with, and us doing it together.

I hope this book gets to be the journey back to YOU. Beautiful, miraculous, incredible you. You, as a powerful manifestor, who has called this book and this moment into your life, because on a soul level you know you are made for more. And although scared or perhaps confused about HOW to make it happen, you are ready for it.

It can be very easy to get caught up in all the reasons you CAN'T have the life that you want. But I want to bring awareness to the fact that there is a person on this planet *right now* who is living the life you want, so why not you?

I feel honored that I get to partner with you on this journey.

Now let's dive in…

Chapter One

One Thought Away

*T*his book is titled *One Thought Away* because what I have found is that most people are just one thought away from making a decision that will move them forward to the life they want, or not.

One thought away is more than a phrase, though—it is a state of mind that leads to a future result. I want to focus you on harnessing the power of that "thought moment," so it is working for you, not against you.

The accumulation of positive thought moments lead to the desired life results you want. Thought by thought, moment by moment, intentional action by intentional action … your dream life becomes a reality–one holy, happy, and healthy thought at a time.

It only takes one thought to step into our next level of potential. That one thought can stretch us outside our comfort zone to see what lies on the other side. I think most things we want are just outside our comfort zone, or else we would already have them.

The human brain is wired to not like uncertainty and change. So when we start to stretch beyond our normal thoughts, feelings, actions, and routines, red flags could go up. What if we didn't equate it to mean that anything was wrong, though? What if we allowed ourselves to understand that we are just interrupting old thoughts, beliefs, feelings, and actions? That we are trying something new, and that could lead to a breakthrough in having next-level results in our life?

Not to mention, research shows that often when we get outside our comfort zone, we realize that the thing we feared is not so scary, after all. That we do have what it takes to do hard things. Things can seem harder because our belief about them is that they must be hard, but once we take them on, we get past a fear zone and enter a growth zone.

An article by Integra Property Services, titled From Comfort Zone to Growth Zone[1], explains that we have four zones. The first one is our Comfort Zone, where we believe we are in control and most comfortable, but where something new rarely happens. The second is our Fear Zone, which is full of the unknown and, therefore, can cause self-doubt and discomfort. The third is our Learning Zone, which is a zone of knowledge and self-discovery that will teach us what we need to know to be successful and broaden our opportunities. Last, we have our Growth Zone, where we reach our goals and fulfill our dreams.

But first, we must have a goal to reach, right? In One Thought Away, our goal is our big dream, the dream that spurs us to take action.

Regardless, we must leave our Comfort Zone and travel through the Fear and Learning Zones before we can arrive at our ultimate destination, the Growth Zone.

The important thing is to take some immediate, inspired action—note that I didn't say perfect action. It's not about doing it perfectly, because perfection is a fairy tale that sets everyone up for failure and can stall them out. Taking immediate, inspired action is critical to move from where you are to where you want to be, though.

---

[1] Integra Property Services, From Comfort Zone to Growth Zone, From comfort zone to growth zone | Integra Property Services (integra-ps.com)

Inspired action is meant to move your life forward to a place that is filled with grace, or unmerited favor from God. It's the place where you get to exhale and realize you may not have all the answers or know how it is going to turn out, but you are willing to see where the forward movement will take you. In that moment, you are at least going for a one percent shift in who you are today, upgrading from who you were yesterday.

Why don't we live this way all the time? The reason is because our brains are innately programmed to equate change to pain. But I'd like to challenge you to consider a different type of thinking. What if we reprogram our thinking to equate change to possibility? And how awesome would it be if, when we got to a moment where change was calling us, we got excited… even if we are nervous?

Going for the Big Goal

Setting goals for yourself is a great thing, it gives your brain something to hook into and work toward. I want to encourage you to stop going for the soft goals, though, meaning goals that you already know you can achieve. Achieving something you know you can do holds little reward.

In the past, perhaps you were scared to go for those stretchier goals because you feared them. You had been conditioned to think it would somehow result in pain … pain of rejection, abandonment, not being good enough … whatever your thought pattern has been up to this point.

If we are now equating change to opportunity, though, that opens up an entirely new future. Let's dive deeper…

I'm inviting you to get out of your comfort zone, open your arms up wide, and reach, really reach for what you want. What do you REALLY WANT in this lifetime?

Is it love? Wealth? Health? Adventure? Play? Where are you still holding back, and let's not forget the big question: WHY? We get one chance at this life; why waste it on just getting by when you could create a massive ripple effect in your joy and fun factor. We could actually manifest and create a life that is beyond your wildest dreams.

A good thing to remember is that there are people *right now* on this planet proving that your dream life is possible, because they are living it! That's great for them ... and why not you? The only difference is that you don't know that you can do it, or you don't know how.

So, what is it that you want? That thing when you get to the end of your life you look back and know you lived a life with no regrets. Is it...

- Launching your own business
- Traveling the world
- Making major improvements to your health
- Getting a degree
- Loving yourself
- Falling in love
- Getting married
- Starting a family
- Moving across the country
- Building your dream home
- Starting a non-profit
- Leaving a legacy

What is it for you? Don't worry about what others say. Put aside what your parents, spouse, siblings, best friend, or whomever else says it should be... what do YOU want?

That's the conversation I want to have with you.

For example, I have a client who was $100k in debt when she first found me and this work. Instead of holding back and saying she was doomed, she chose to buckle down and learn the One Thought Away Process. She was clear that having that level of debt was not in her "dream life" plan.

So, she committed to working on herself and focused on upleveling her self-mastery skills.

In a short amount of time, she began to transform, which resulted in her finances transforming, too. Her finances were a direct reflection of what she thought she was worthy of and what she felt she was allowed to have.

In a matter of only a few years, she shared with me that she was looking at investing in commercial real estate because she now had so much money, she wanted to spend it wisely, so it would create more income for her.

Her wealth increased on the outside, because she did the work on the inside. She changed what she believed could be possible for her and who she wanted to be, and her bank account reflected that upgrade. She wasn't able to fully understand where her current results were coming from, though, until she did this work.

Where are Your Current Results Coming From?

This is where you get to take an honest inventory of what is not working in your life, so you can address it and make a change once and for all. It's a change that could catapult your life forward. Is it…

- You want more money?
- You want better health?
- You want to find love?
- You want happier relationships?

Instead of overwhelming yourself that you must go from zero to 100% overnight, in regard to attaining your desires, what if you allowed yourself to make a 1% shift every day? That would be a 7% shift by the end of this week! A 30% shift by the end of the month!

Let's say you didn't do it perfectly and some days were really hard, and you feel you went 1% backward versus forward? Maybe you did that 50 days out of the year. You would still have a 315% shift by the end of the year! That would be an INCREDIBLE result!

A starting point to get this 1% increase a day is to jump on the opportunity to take full ownership of all the results you have in your life, and all the results you don't have.

What could you own differently that could help influence a different result? What thoughts could you change? What action could you take that could be different?

Here is the thing that I see holds a lot of people back from even creating a 1% daily change in their lives…

They don't believe they are capable of it. What I have come to find is that what we believe we can accomplish often stems from the ages of 3-8 years old. During these influential years, we have been told or overheard things about us that shaped how we thought about ourselves.

Or perhaps something was done to us that shaped how we thought about ourselves…

Perhaps it was the experience of not being picked up right away when you were a crying baby … you might have made up a story about nobody caring about you.

Or maybe as a kid you had the experience of not being a part of the "in crowd"… and your story ended up being that you weren't good enough.

Or perhaps you didn't get good grades … and you made up a story that you weren't smart enough to get ahead.

Sometimes, the story you tell yourself is based on what someone else said. If you're being told that you need to be "fixed," it could be that something isn't wrong with you at all. Sometimes, there is healing yet to be done in the other person. Perhaps they feel *their* life isn't what they want it to be, and they are projecting that onto you, because they have not yet done their own inner work.

We all have had negative stories about ourselves at some point—we're not popular, not good enough, not smart enough, not pretty enough, not as interesting as others. Your story is holding you back. And whatever is holding you back, there's a story.

But why? Why are we the first ones to jump to the head of the line to beat ourselves up and put ourselves down?

Why are we so loyal to painful beliefs about ourselves?

> "Your story is holding you back. And whatever is holding you back, there's a story."

When we first came into this world as a beautiful little baby, none of those thoughts were in our mind at all. They happened over time, because we didn't have the skill set to understand that we were being influenced to think of ourselves negatively. And since we didn't have an awareness as to what was happening, we let it happen.

Unfortunately, this not knowing has sent millions of people down a rabbit hole where they indulge in not believing in themselves, self-sabotaging, holding back, and ultimately living lives that just don't light them up.

In other words, they end up robbing themselves of the very joy that they wish they had.

Regardless of your story or the reason for it, if you think there's something wrong with you for any reason and there are things you'd love to change, it's time for an honest conversation about facing them and changing them for good.

This is why I am so glad that we get to be here together now. I believe it is never too late to create a different result in your life, no matter what your current age, size, gender, economic or political status, or anything else that you may consciously or unconsciously grasp onto and let get in the way.

You Have a Choice

There is something I know now that I didn't know back when I was a victim of my thoughts:

Being humans, our God Almighty has given us the gift of CHOICE. Moment by moment, we are allowed to *choose* what we want to think of ourselves. Those choices are 100% impacting the life we have right now, and the life we want to have but don't yet.

I am offering you a way out of the confusion, chaos, and overwhelm and into a stance of grounded empowerment, faith, and trust.

This doesn't need to take decades of rehashing your childhood story, but it will demand of you something different that was not demanded of you to get to where you are today.

It's okay, breathe. I've got you.

Think of me as your new best friend, and, together, we are not only going to turn around the parts of your life that aren't feeling great right now, but we are going to call in what would feel extraordinary.

Will it be easy? Some of it might; some of it may not. Will it take work? Yes. But honestly, who cares? This is your life we are talking about! Your life is worth giving it everything you've got.

On the flip side of the coin, if you decide to sit on the fence and think the thoughts that are defeating you for another week, month, year, THREE YEARS or more, you know what's at risk?

Everything.

Everything that you are saying is important to you…

- All those images that you scotch taped and glued to your vision board for all these years.

- All the feelings that you felt in your visualizations of your future.
- All the prayers that you dropped down to your knees to ask for.
- All the dreams and the "I wish that was me's" that you said along the way.

All of it.

Here's how I see it…

You have nothing to lose and everything to gain by giving the One Thought Away Process your all. What does that mean? It means we lock arms and get super focused and intentional about your life.

I'm not talking about being focused in a way that you rub the genie lamp and ask for something you want, let's say weight loss. But then you sit on the couch and eat a bag of chips every night and wonder why weight loss isn't happening for you.

No, I'm being real. I'm talking about being focused in the way you set a strong intention. Then you get into massive, fierce, committed *action* to make that weight loss vision happen for you.

What I know to be true is that if something is really important to us, we will do whatever it takes to make it happen. I have seen it thousands of times with my clients. I also know from my own experience in living a life of ups and downs myself.

But what if that WHY isn't strong enough? Then the day that it's rainy outside, or you get a flat tire, or have a big deadline at work … the day that additional stress hits your plate, you will throw everything out the window and revert to old thoughts and ways of being. At some point, you'll resentfully wonder why life never worked out for you.

The old way of being is easier to choose when life feels tough, because it's what you currently KNOW. It's called your comfort zone. But everything you want is just outside your comfort zone, all tied up with a glamorous, fantastic shiny bow, just waiting for you to do what it takes to claim it.

So, you can stay in your comfort zone, avoiding stretching yourself to the next level. Or you can stretch yourself outside of your comfort zone, where your dream life is waiting for you.

Are you going to turn your back on that dream life, or are you going to go after it with everything you've got and claim it for your own?

You CAN do this! It is within your reach!

And that is exactly the work that we get to do together. We're going to be two new besties, rolling up our sleeves and breathing life into the dreams you are saying are important to you.

It is time to let go of all the excuses, so you never need to wonder *what if*. Someday you will find yourself on your deathbed (I'm not being morbid, but it is science based that we are all headed there), and my stand for you is that you won't be looking back on your life with any regrets.

Your life is not a dress rehearsal. Time is the one thing you can for sure never get back, so why not be *all in?*

That's what you have to do if you want to live the life of your dreams. You have to go all in and be your biggest cheerleader and believer, rooting yourself on from start to finish. If you have big dreams, you can't play small.

It doesn't seem that drinking excessive amounts of green juice, wearing only fair-trade cotton clothing, and eating only organic foods is enough. Although all of that is great, it's not moving the needle forward to you hitting your big dream goals.

What will?

The One Thought Away Process...

- **Mindset Mastery:** This means knowing how to create neuroconnections in your brain that are positive. In other words, training your brain to see the cup is overflowing, versus being half empty. Without this in place, it is very easy to slide back into the old story of what isn't working for you.

- **Emotional Mastery:** Gaining skills to be able to witness and sit with your emotions and not be overcome by them. This includes emotions that are hard, like fear, stress, anxiety, jealousy, and anger. It's not just about the hard emotions, though; it also includes the ones you desire, like joy, without fearing it will go away and you won't be able to attain it again. Part of this skill set is realizing your emotions are energy and getting curious as to what information they have to give you. This helps you determine if you are on or off track with your values and goals.

- **Relationship to Self:** Your relationship to yourself is a foundational piece of transforming your life. How you treat yourself daily is a building block to everything else. It's about getting your relationship to yourself to a place where you love, honor, respect, and adore yourself, no matter what.

- **Becoming and Staying Present:** This step is all about letting go of the way you check out, escape, or numb out from your emotions, experiences, people, or life in general. Everyone has a vice at some point of their lives ... could be food, alcohol, social media, shopping, work, gambling, or smoking, just to name a few. Letting go of vices and staying present to the moment gives you an opportunity to stop living in the past, which is often fear based, and stop living in the future, which is often worry based. It is an opportunity to become present to the NOW moment and make healthy decisions to create happy moments right now.

- **Learning to Sustain the Transformation:** Unless you lock in the skills to sustain your transformation, your growth could be a short hit of relief, versus a real change. Transformation is not about taking a magic pill that doesn't have lasting results. It's not about being given a fish, but rather about learning how to fish. Mastering yourself is mastering your life.

This is where it gets even more fun...

Manifesting Your Results

Now here's the thing, there are infinite possibilities that are out there for each of us in regard to where we can choose to take our lives. And God has given us the power of CHOICE to put our attention, efforts, and energy on the ones that light us up.

Do you want an unhealthy body?
Nope ... pass on that option.

Do you want difficult friendships?
No, thank you. Pass.

Do you want a loving relationship with your family?
Heck, yes, choose that possibility.

Do you want tons of money to do whatever you want?
Of course, put that one on your dance card.

Manifesting starts with how you *think*, and this is the part where so many people miss out.

I have a great life. I have been very intentional in creating it. It's not perfect, I'm not perfect. But the work we are going to do in this book is the very work I have personally used to create an incredible life. I now catch myself as quickly as possible if I'm off course and course correct when I have veered too far off track.

One of the tools I use is visualization. I find that in visualizing what I want my life to look like, and *feeling* what it feels like to have already attained it, I'm branding the assumption of that life into my brain. I am creating and reinforcing neural pathways in my brain, training it to assume that is the life I get to live today.

The feeling part of this process is important. What will it feel like to have that life? How will I feel when I have attained it? I start to feel the joy of having that reality NOW. It's something my body, mind, and soul start to assume is going to happen. I get intentional about thinking and feeling like a woman who has that life already.

This is one of the steps that you can choose to master, so you, too, can break the thinking and feelings that got yesterday's results that did not work for you.

A good habit is to bookend your days with a visualization ritual based on the life that you are committed to creating. When you do that, you will naturally start to take actions that are going to support that vision. Your brain will be trained to assume that's where you're headed.

Over time, with the help of what you will learn in this book, you will start to take actions without needing to think about them. Those natural actions will support your vision coming true.

This book includes some visualizations for you, which you can access at www.OneThoughtAwayBook.com/Bonus. When you go into your visualizations, allow yourself to get excited. Don't come at it as a "chore" you have to do. You don't "have" to do anything. You GET to do this; you are BLESSED to do these visualizations and create the life you want from a place of grace, ease, and flow.

Your visualizations are a desirable place to be, and by being there, you create desirable feelings. This produces feel-good chemicals in your brain, called dopamine and serotonin, that lift your energy and perspective about your life and the world around you.

I believe that your personal development work, the work that you are doing here with me right now, is the most powerful work you could ever do in your life. It will help you refocus your energy and bring your light back up if it's dimmed.

This book gets to be an anchor for you to feel plugged into the work we are doing together. If you're feeling doubtful, scared, confused, or you're having a hard day, you can pull out this book or connect to the One Thought Away Community in our private Facebook group. You can find that group here: *(www.facebook.com/groups/onethoughtawayproject)*.

These steps can act as anchors to take your life to the next level, to have it feel better than it does today. This is called anchoring. An anchor is when we can instantly bring ourselves back to a positive moment in order to shift your emotional state.

An opening to freedom is being together, even beyond this book. Engage with us on the online forum, join one of our coaching programs for women, or form your own book club with your friends, or in your church or other organizations.

With this book, you will learn to process and integrate. You will start to feel loved, seen, heard, and understood like you haven't before. You will expose what you don't like and what isn't working, so you can clearly see and claim what you desire and what is rightfully yours.

My Hidden Shame

I protected my disorder for decades. I closed the doors and curtains so people couldn't see the crazy ways I was behaving when alone in my home. I had shame, and I was embarrassed that I was dealing with it.

A part of me felt like eating food should be something that is so basic, and I had somehow messed it all up. I didn't even know what a normal portion size was anymore and couldn't connect to my body to know if it was truly physically hungry. I felt that I should be able to break the addictive cycle, but I kept stumbling.

Here's the thing, though, it was never about food and eating in the first place. Those were just symptoms of something deeper going on. Deeper was the fact that I did not have skills to shift my thoughts and feelings to work for me, not against me.

It wasn't until I allowed myself to be supported by another person who was skilled to help me, that I could really start to break the chains that those old beliefs had on me.

It wasn't until I slowed down and got curious and interested with my thoughts and feelings that I could change anything at all. I asked myself the important question: WHY do I want to transform in the first place?

This is a powerful moment where you can ask yourself the number one thing you're committed to shifting from reading this book. Take a breath, get grounded, connect with yourself, and then write it down in a journal or on a piece of paper. This starts with believing that you can do it—you can achieve your goals and make your dream life come true.

And believing starts in one place—our thoughts. One thought can be the catalyst that changes your life. To put those thoughts into action and give them fuel, it's important to visualize what your life, your goal, will look like once it becomes reality.

As they say, seeing is believing, so I would like to gift you a visualization to help you see, in your mind's eye, what you want to create in your life. The more you train your mind to see what you want, and feel as if it is already yours, the faster you bring it into reality. So, don't put off this next step. Enjoy this gift now...

Please listen now at: www.OneThoughtAwayBook.com/Bonus

I would love to hear from you on the One Thought Away online community how your first visualization was, so ask to join now and let's go!

Chapter Two

Thought Swap

"*I* just don't know how I can make it work. I feel I can't add one more thing, even though I know working on myself would change my life."

"Pam, I'm standing for you to see you can have it all, when you shift your mindset and get into different actions."

"I just don't know how to even begin."

"I get that, but don't let excuses stand in the way of your joy. I can help."

Pam's mindset is one that I have heard a thousand times. A mindset that there is not enough time, especially for anything that would make her happy. She had trained herself to put everyone and everything before her own needs, and last on the list was getting her nowhere fast.

That first conversation with Pam was hard for her. Sometimes it is hard to get honest with ourselves about things we aren't proud of. Ignoring them does not get us ahead, though.

The clients who have joined our community know they are one thought away from having the life they want… or not. And what to do about it.

Pam didn't take joining our community seriously at first. When she met us, she was in her late 60s, and by first appearances, she had it all together. At the time, she worked for one of the largest software companies in the world and had an incredible career.

She also had 5 kids, 20 grandkids, and had been happily married in her second marriage for more than 20 years. She had a full life, a large family, and a great marriage. A lot of people would think Pam had it all.

But internally, she wasn't happy. She didn't feel good about herself, and she was not comfortable in her body. She had self-esteem issues and, although it appeared she had a successful life and career, Pam was uneasy with where she was in her life.

There were things she wanted to change.

When I talked to Pam about joining our women's group coaching program, however, she declined. There just wasn't enough time. She didn't have enough money. What she did have plenty of, though, were excuses. Of course, I respected her decision. After all, this was her choice to make.

In the next five months, things got significantly worse for Pam. Her weight became more of an issue, and she was more uncomfortable with her health and her body. Work had become increasingly more difficult, and her overall joy factor had declined. Pam finally admitted that if she wanted to turn her life around, she needed help. I helped her understand that asking for help was a sign of strength, not weakness.

When she stopped making excuses and went all in with her inner work, Pam was shocked at how quickly her life changed. She lost her unwanted weight, created financial abundance through an unprecedented retirement program, and for the first time, she and her husband took vacations and went on cruises.

In the past, it was a life she never dreamed she would live, but she came in and did the One Thought Away Process, and here she is now loving her life. To top it off she has started a passion career in her 70s doing the work she really loves, coaching women to their own amazing transformations.

Pam happily shares her story with people, telling them not to wait and let their excuses stand in their way of the life they want to create. As she says, she lost five months because she was looking for reasons not to create change, rather than being all in to the life she really wanted and getting our support to make it happen.

Five months is a long time to be unhappy at work. It's a long time to be uncomfortable in your own skin. It's far too long to rob yourself of the joy you deserve.

And I have to wonder, what could Pam have done in those five months had she not waited?

We'll never know.

But we do know that it doesn't have to take you five more months to choose something better for your own life. It only takes one thought to make different decisions and choices, starting today.

Like Pam, you can stop making excuses and give yourself permission to transform your life. Whatever your dream is, it is just one thought away.

The Importance of One Thought Away

What is One Thought Away? One Thought Away is a process and a practice that can help you create your dream life. It is where the solutions you've been searching for reside. And it's where you can discover how to unlock your ability to overcome your insecurities, challenges, fears, and self-sabotaging behaviors.

After working with hundreds of people, I have seen time and again that the answer to people's struggles and fears is in their thoughts and how they are using their minds. The mind is one of the most powerful tools we have, and our thoughts are the most important influencers in every action we take and every decision we make.

Why is One Thought Away important? It's important because the way you're thinking is defining your results. You'll continue to get the results you've always gotten if you continue to think the way you've always thought. Nothing changes unless it first changes in your thoughts and your mind, which starts with a DECISION to change it.

Now, think about it. If the way you think defines your results, isn't it just as true that your thoughts ultimately define your life?

I'm living proof that my internal thoughts got me to a very unhealthy place, but One Thought Away was a foundational piece to my transformation.

It can be in yours, too.

If it's that simple, you might wonder why so many people are plagued with insecurities, fears, anxiety, stress, you name it. The truth is, most people are not leveraging the potential of their mind. And as a result, they're limiting themselves to a life that is far less than what they are capable of living.

Claiming What is Rightfully Yours

Unfortunately, many people go through their entire life without experiencing the life they've always wanted to live.

This was proven in a 2020 study, when Daniel Pink conducted the World Regret Project, which is the largest analysis of international attitudes about regret. The project analyzed more than 15,000 regrets from people living in 105 different countries. The study revealed that more than 80 percent of the global participants had experienced regret, either occasionally or frequently.

According to Pink, "In the world of work ... [sometimes] you're at a juncture in your life [where] you can play it safe [or] you can take the chance — and people play it safe," he said. "And then they regret it".[2]

It's worth mentioning that his statement could apply to so much more than work. There's no denying that often we play it safe when it comes to any risky or life-changing decision.

Pink also states that what we regret the most reveals what we value the most.

But you don't have to spend your life regretting what could have been. Starting right now, you can take a stand for yourself and claim the dream life that is rightfully yours.

> You can choose to be the victor who creates the thoughts, and commands the up-leveled life, that you've only previously dared to envision.

What this means is you can stay in the old thought patterns that have held you back and kept you in struggle. Or you can choose to be the victor who creates the new thoughts, and commands the up-leveled life, that you've only previously dared to envision.

Even better, you can choose to do it in a way where it can actually be fun for you. I'm not saying it's always gonna be fun. We all know that transformation requires growth, and sometimes growing pains can be hard, but don't let it scare you. My experience has been that, in the long run, it is always worth it.

I also encourage you to not think of your personal development journey as "work" as much as it is a lifestyle. It is not a to-do list of all the things you must check off. It is a way of being, believing and broadcasting your

---

[2] Pepper, F, Ferguson, Z (2022) Regret is a Very Common Emotion, ABC News, https://www.abc.net.au/news/2022-03-03/learning-from-regret-daniel-pink-this-working-life/100848018

dreams into the world.

And your dreams are your lifelines for your soul.

They are what gets you excited to wake up in the morning, looking forward to what the day will bring. Your dreams hold your passions, and even more, they are what can make you passionate about your career, your hobbies, the people you love, the causes you support, and, yes, the life you live.

That's what dreams have the capability to do. And that's why I encourage you to dream big. Go all out and reach for the stars! Why? Because you can.

Many people are afraid to dream big, so they settle. They settle for less than what they want, less than what they deserve, and less than what they are capable of creating.

There are common fears that come up when we dare to dream and live bigger. Some of the common fears are:

Common Fears to Disrupt:

- What if I fail?
- What if I'm not qualified?
- What if I don't deserve this?
- What will others think or say?
- What if there's more to lose?
- What if it doesn't happen? Then what am I going to do?
- I don't have the money.
- I don't have the time.
- What if I'm not happy, even when I've achieved what I want.
- Will others think I'm too old? Too young? Too anything?
- What if I disappoint myself?
- What if I hurt myself?
- I feel vulnerable, and I don't like that feeling.

- How do I know this will really work for me?
- How can I trust this person has my best interest at heart?

These fears start as self-sabotaging thoughts that keep us from moving forward. Let's look at a tool that can help shift the way of thinking that is holding you back. Let's talk about flipping perceptions, a process I like to call Thought Swap.

Flipping Perceptions

When you look at that list above, you can see that they are stemming from a fear-based mindset. A mindset that is sending out fear-based *thoughts*. Thoughts that keep our dreams away from us.

Studies show that the things we fear in our heads often don't come true, even though we have played out the fear thousands of times in our heads. One particular study by Penn State University, titled Exposing Worry's Deceit: Percentage of Untrue Worries in Generalized Anxiety Disorder Treatment, shows that 91 percent of the participants' worries did not come to fruition.

So, these fear-based thoughts are nothing more than perceptions, and perceptions can be changed.

Change your perceptions; change your thoughts; change your life. How do you do that? You flip your perceptions. You change, or swap, your thoughts so they are positive and gear your mind toward favorable outcomes, rather than preconceived negative outcomes.

Flipping your perceptions is an exercise of opposites, flipping the viewpoint of a thought to the opposite viewpoint. Not only is it positive and enlightening, but it's kind of fun.

Let's get started. Let's do a Thought Swap.

Thought: What if it doesn't work out?
Swapped thought: What if it works out better than I ever imagined?

Thought: What if I'm too old?
Swapped Thought: What if I'm the perfect age for this?

Thought: What if it's overwhelming?
Swapped Thought: What if it's easier than I think?

Thought: What if I disappoint myself?
Swapped Thought: What if I surprise myself?

Thought: I don't have the time.
Swapped thought: I can make time for this; it's that important to me.

Thought: This is scary. I'm afraid.
Swapped thought: I might discover there's nothing to be afraid of!

I think you get the idea. It's a game of what ifs ... outcomes that are made up in our own minds. Our fears are often worst-case possibilities conjured up by our thoughts. But by flipping our perceptions from worst-case to best-case, our outlook could drastically change. In doing so, we may release our fears altogether, or at least de-charge them a bit.

Let's imagine you find yourself teetering on the edge of a ski slope, knowing that there's only one way down. But you're afraid to push off. You fear this isn't going to end well.

But what if you are surprised to discover that you love the exhilarating feeling of skiing down that slope? By the time you get to the bottom, you're so proud and excited that you want to get back up to the top and do it all over again!

"Oh my gosh, I did it!"

That's a common reaction when you face your fear. You open up to a new experience. It also opens a new way of thinking and allows for a shift in perception from "No way!" to "Wahoooo, let's do this!"

It's your choice. You're one thought away from being stuck in a fear cycle. Or one thought away from living a life you have been dreaming of. And that dream life is often not really that far off, except in your head.

So, are your thoughts going to control you? Or are you ready to control your thoughts?

One Thought Away

THOUGHT SWAPS

Print out this worksheet and hang it where you can see it on a daily basis. Surround yourself with new ideas and perceptions. Get into the habit of being an optimist about your life and world.

Change your perceptions; change your thoughts; change your life.

Swapping your thoughts is an exercise of opposites, swapping the standpoint of a thought to the opposite standpoint. Not only is it positive and enlightening, but it's kind of fun. Let's get started. Let's do a Thought Swap.

1 Thought: What if it doesn't work out?
Swapped thought: What if it works out better than I ever imagined?

2 Thought: What if I'm too old?
Swapped Thought: What if I'm the perfect age for this?

3 Thought: What if it's overwhelming?
Swapped Thought: What if it's easier than I think?

4 Thought: What if I disappoint myself?
Swapped Thought: What if I surprise myself?

5 Thought: I don't have the time.
Swapped thought: I can make time for this; it's that important to me.

6 Thought: This is scary. I'm afraid.
Swapped thought: I might discover there's nothing to be afraid of!

#onethoughtaway | support@kerrytepedino.com | www.onethoughtawaybook.com

Chapter Three

The Stories We Tell Ourselves

"Grandma would have been so proud of you," I told Barack Obama when I met him in San Francisco.

"Thank you so much. That means so much to me," he replied as he leaned in and gave me a hug.

Meeting Barack Obama when he was a presidential candidate was unforgettable to me. But it was my grandmother who met him first.

My grandma, Mabel Hefty, lived in Hawaii, and in Hawaiian, Tutu means grandma. Tutu was beautiful inside and out, and a powerhouse teacher who taught fifth grade at Punahou, which is a school on Oahu.

And as his book tells, Barack Obama was her student. He still today often refers to her on Teacher Appreciation Day as the most influential teacher that he has had. With all of his high school teachers and big university professors, it was Tutu who left a lasting impression on the child who would later become our country's first black president.

He speaks about how she impacted and influenced him to be proud of the person he is. As a student in 5th grade, he was at an age when many children struggle with their self-esteem. They compare themselves to their classmates, often finding fault in themselves or differences that make them stand out or feel inferior.

As President Obama tells it, he said he felt different from his peers right away, mostly because of his African heritage. He looked different than the rest of his class, and he felt different, but not in a good way. In the fifth grade, Barack Obama wanted to be like everyone else and fit in.

Coincidentally, my grandmother had once lived in Kenya, where she also taught school, and she brought that culture and heritage into her home. When I grew up, there were tribal masks on her walls and zebra drums in her house, and I'd often look at them and fantasize what it would be like to live in Africa.

Since Tutu was so fond of Africa, when she found out that Barack was from there, she was thrilled. She had become very attached to Africa, the tribes, her students there, and the people she had grown to love.

So when she found out that Barack's father was coming to Hawaii to visit, which he did only once, she invited him to speak to all the fifth-grade classes about where he came from. She wanted her students to learn about the heritage and experience the beauty of Kenya. She welcomed stories from Barack's father, not only as an educational lesson, but also to help her students understand and appreciate the country.

When Barack's father walked into the classroom, the students listened intently as he shared colorful stories, painting a picture of a land and lifestyle that were foreign to them. The kids absolutely loved it.

Even more, Barack, who had struggled with his heritage and being different from his peers, benefitted as much, if not more, than his fellow classmates. He started to feel pride about where he was from and who he was, in a way he hadn't before.

The future president remembered my tutu well when I met him at the San Francisco fundraiser.

I was among a large crowd that had been waiting for him for quite a long time. As he entered the room the crowd pressed forward to get near him. I was six rows back, trying as hard as I could to edge myself closer to the red velvet rope, with no luck. He was coming closer to where I was, and I knew I did not have much time to get on his radar.

So, I quickly turned to the young man next to me, and said, "I promise you he will stop in front of us if you yell, 'Mabel Hefty's granddaughter' as loud as you can to get his attention."

The young man looked at me as if I was crazy, decided he had nothing to lose and joined in on my efforts. But Barack passed us without stopping.

I was shocked. Immediately I thought to myself, "Why did I come this far if I am not to meet him? This doesn't make sense to me."

And all of a sudden, like an afterthought, he stopped and backtracked and came back to where I was. The crowd parted, and I walked to the front and reached out to him. He took my hand and pulled me in for a hug. We spoke briefly and shared a special moment centered around a woman we both loved. She had impacted both of us greatly, influencing each of us to who we are today.

Later, I was sitting on a bench in the hotel lobby, sharing with my friend my experience. She said she had met him, too. She told him that she was at the fundraiser with me, Mabel Hefty's granddaughter. He replied he knew who I was and that we had just spoken.

Not long after, I received a personal letter on White House letterhead from President Barack Obama. It spoke in beautiful detail about how grateful he was for my grandmother and how much she meant to him.

President Obama has given my tutu credit and kudos for her part in influencing him. I wonder if he hadn't had her support and understanding, would he have stepped into being the man he is today and who he was as president. One only needs to read his book, or listen to him relate stories of his past, to know that he now embraces his heritage and the role it has played in his career and life.

I'm sure it impacted him to become the man that he was for all of us as president. One only needs to read his book or listen to him relate stories of his past to know that he now embraces his heritage and the role it has played in his career.

As I mentioned earlier, we have all struggled with who we are at some point in our lives. Usually, it starts at an early age. We feel we are too tall, too short, too heavy, too skinny, too smart, not smart enough, too poor, too shy, too awkward.

As we grow up, we can have a tendency to let those inferiorities and self-doubts build on themselves, and their impact on our life intensifies—unless we get the mindset training to take ourself out of old stories and labels that aren't working for us and into ones that will.

What's Your Story?

Can you relate to fifth-grade Barack Obama?

Think about young Barack—what beliefs, false or otherwise, did he have about himself? What was likely his mindset before his father visited his school?

Can you relate to his thoughts about not wanting to be different or not feeling comfortable being yourself?

At one time or another, most of us have felt that we didn't really fit in. We might have believed that others were negatively judging us for our differences. That we didn't matter, or that our opinion was not valued.

Those feelings can be so overwhelming that they seem insurmountable at the time.

But they aren't. Barack Obama is a great example of how we can turn our thoughts of shame to acceptance, embracing our differences, rather than distancing ourselves from them.

And that feeling is freeing!

It is also just one thought away.

Imagine what Barack's life would be today if it hadn't been for one thought … my grandmother having the thought of inviting his father to speak to the classroom … his father having the thought to accept that invitation … and Barack allowing himself to think positively about his heritage and his differences.

In that instance, one thought didn't just change one person. It very likely was so significant that it impacted an entire country, perhaps the entire world!

Now, perhaps the beliefs we have about ourselves aren't impacting a whole world, but they can be just as limiting. Let's take a look at some I hear often…

Common Beliefs to Disrupt:

- I'm not enough.
- People will judge me.
- Being different is bad.

We've all grown up with some version of these insecurities and fears. The problem is most of us believed them at some point. We bought into those beliefs, no matter how much truth was lacking behind them. But that doesn't mean that we were at fault. Far from it.

Your beliefs are usually the result of something that happened in your childhood, likely between the formative years of three and eight. This is when children are easily influenced by something someone said, or an experience that made them feel that they were different. As the years went on, you most likely held onto those beliefs and allowed them to take seed and grow.

Let me ask, though, how is it going to serve us to continue to believe those stories and thoughts? Yet, we let them take up residence in our heads and affect the opinions we have of ourselves. Again, I ask, why? What purpose does this serve, other than to create a false reality that we are, indeed, less than, not worthy, and different in a negative way?

What if you start to form a different sense of self, like Barack did that day, when he allowed himself to entertain a different perspective? He rattled the foundation that he had built that he was different, not good enough, and didn't fit in with the rest of the kids. All it took was one rattle to begin the process that would eventually break up and crumble that limiting belief.

Think of a foundation under a house that has one job—to support the entire structure and keep it whole. All it takes is one crack to weaken that foundation to the point where it will eventually crumble the whole structure.

Barack Obama built a new foundation under his feet. He began to believe in himself and transition his thoughts from negative to positive. Instead of feeling vastly different, he accepted a new belief, that his differences were special.

This new foundation accepted and approved of his uniqueness. It left him with the belief that his heritage had value, and because of them, he could make an impact on others.

By changing his thoughts, he built a new foundation, on which he built a new house and a new life, one for the history books.

It is possible that it was a pivotal day that changed the course of his life and the history that he made.

How did it actually happen? Barack Obama formed different neural connections in his brain. In doing so, he wrote a different story about his value, worth, background, family, and history. As a result, he did things historically that our government had never seen before.

You can do that, too. You can take on a different perspective about yourself, in turn start to write a different story about your life. A story of you creating your dream life.

What are the stories that you're telling yourself right now about who you are?

Are you afraid of being judged like Barack Obama was? Why? Where does it stem from as a child? Perhaps you overheard someone say something when they didn't realize you were within earshot. And now as an adult you may be still judging yourself based on someone else's opinion from way back when you were a child.

Here's the deal; our subconscious remembers those things and wants to protect us from pain. So it keeps those memories at the forefront, saying, "Hey, remember what so and so said and how much it hurt? You don't want that to happen again, so don't put yourself out there fully in front of others."

This is called confirmation bias, and we often resort to it in decision making. By referring to our past experiences, we receive validation that we are making the right decision in the present moment.

But are we? Not when we can see confirmation bias as a thinking shortcut to prove we are right. When we strive to seek validation, we are blinded to what might not be working that we want to change. As a result, we hold back from our next level of potential, buying into our limiting, negative beliefs.

Instead of changing our thoughts, we choose to live with them and let them wreak havoc on us, possibly for the rest of our lives.

But we don't have to do that! We can switch our thoughts to create different beliefs—beliefs that can totally change our outcomes and our lives.

Lessons to Learn:

- I'm already enough, even as I continue to grow and transform.
- What other people think of me is none of my business. Knowing I'm a person of integrity is what matters.
- If everyone were the same, life would be boring. I love being unique!

Imagine a life where you get to celebrate you and all that you are and can be. Imagine a life where you get to shine your light brightly, instead of living in the shadows of your own potential.

Shine Your Light

It's your turn to shine. You can roll up your sleeves and do some fun and deep work. Believe me, it's worth it!

Until you uncover and heal the beliefs about yourself that are holding you back, you'll remain unconsciously loyal to them.

If you think about it, it would be staying loyal to dimming your light, rather than stepping into your power. It would be choosing to play small, versus going for the vision you have for your life. I say, let's show up and play full out; that's the only way you're going to win.

That's what one of my clients, Laura, did. She admits that she had a fear of judgment and believes it came from having a mother who was extremely critical. Making it worse, she didn't have a lot of friends in grade school. With just one friend to confide in, she found that her secrets were being shared.

As a child, that can be devastating. It left her feeling very vulnerable. For decades, she held back from allowing herself to develop strong relationships in fear of being hurt. She did not trust many people, and she held herself back.

Laura's life was doomed to feel like a constant struggle if she didn't do the personal development work to change her view of herself. Laura did the hard work to stop fearing other people's judgment. She got focused on her Relationship to Self, which is step three of the One Thought Away Process.

Laura now feels safe in being vulnerable with people that she can trust. She understands that even though she had painful experiences in her childhood, she doesn't have to keep reliving that fear of being judged or betrayed today.

Laura has done the hard work and has proven to herself that she can have a positive view of herself. She now knows that there can be a positive outcome and experience when she's vulnerable. Even though these things happened to her as a child, it doesn't mean that she needs to keep believing she isn't worthy or people can't be trusted.

I helped Laura understand that being the best version of herself in that moment didn't mean that she would need to be perfect. Nobody is. But she could commit to doing the best she can, and even when she slipped up, she could always course correct.

Laura now has a skillset where she feels safe creating close relationships. She has learned to use discretion and create healthy boundaries. She understands what she brings to the table in relationships and is proud of who she is.

She did have to work on herself, though. She could have continued to live in fear and keep people at arm's distance. But she CHOSE to do the work and, in turn, has created an incredible life for herself.

By reframing that she didn't "have to" do something, she actually took her power back and started to own her results in an entirely different way.

The truth is, you don't HAVE to do anything either. You GET to do this work on yourself, if you choose. You are blessed to do this work, if you choose—blessed to gain skills that will help you create the life you want.

This, of course, takes conscious effort, and it is a choice. Choose to acknowledge your beliefs and fears. Then choose to accept that you are one thought away from changing those fears and beliefs so they work for you, not against you.

You can give yourself permission to think differently than you have before. What if you allowed yourself to believe it is safe to discover the beliefs that are holding you back and how they got there?

Your life is worth it; you are worth it. This is some of the most important work you can do in your life, because nothing shifts unless you go all the way with it.

Laura felt like she couldn't trust anyone. The good thing was that she proved that wrong. Now she knows that she has what it takes to use wise discretion. Today, she trusts herself to set healthy boundaries.

The key for Laura was to know that she was safe to trust others with her innermost thoughts and feelings. Little Laura didn't feel safe, and that feeling would continue to shake the foundation of all of her relationships, until she was able to replace it with a more secure feeling. Until she learned that she could trust those who were trustworthy. Now that Laura feels happy and healthy, those in her inner circle win, too, with a deeper and more significant connection to her.

Like Laura and the young Barack Obama, the stories of our youth influence us to be who we are today. We can choose today who we want to be as people we respect in the world and what we want our lives to look like. Just because we created a story long ago is no reason to hang onto it.

We have the power and the ability to rewrite the stories that aren't working for us.

The new story of your life can be as big as you want it to be. It can be a masterpiece. It can be historic. It could even be a story fit for a president.

This is what we call the art of writing a different story.

One Thought Away

THE STORIES WE TELL OURSELVES

Your beliefs are most likely the result of something that happened in your childhood, likely between the formative years of three and eight. Often children are influenced by something they heard or an experience they had, that made them feel different or not good enough. As the years went on, if healing work had not been done, then those beliefs may have grown stronger.

What are the stories that you're telling yourself right now about who you are?

1 Common Belief To Disrupt: I'm not enough.
Lesson To Learn: I'm already enough, even as I continue to grow and transform.

2 Common Belief To Disrupt: People will judge me.
Lesson To Learn: What other people think of me is none of my business. Knowing I'm a person of integrity is what matters.

3 Common Belief To Disrupt: Being different is bad.
Lesson To Learn: If everyone were the same, life would be boring! I love being unique!

#onethoughtaway | support@kerrytepedino.com | www.onethoughtawaybook.com

Chapter Four

That's Not My Underwear!

"What in the world is this?!"

My head was spinning at what I'd found, and as soon as I realized the only possible conclusion to be drawn, my heart sunk.

Five months before our wedding, I got into bed and I felt something at my feet. The bed was made, everything seemed as if it was in place, "What could it be?" I wondered. I managed to grab whatever it was with my feet and pull it up, so I could grab it with my hand.

What I found changed my life.

A pair of green thong underwear, and they weren't mine. I called my fiancé into the room and confronted him, hoping there was some reasonable explanation.

"What's this?" I demanded to know.

At the time, I was helping raise two little girls, and he immediately saw that he had an excuse in them.

"That must be the girls' underwear," he said.

At the time, the girls were three and five years old. They wore cute children's cotton underwear with little Cinderellas and princesses on them, and while this thong underwear was small, it definitely was not little girl panties.

When I called him on it, he tried to fumble his way out of the obvious accusation. He was clearly flustered, and I could tell he was guilty. The cat was out of the bag, and his secret had been found out.

While I tried to wrap my head around the situation, it occurred to me that this woman, whoever she was, had to know that she wasn't wearing her panties when she walked out of our house.

Not only did she know that she'd left behind a souvenir for one of us to find, but she wanted him to get caught.

In the heat of the moment, I knew I had to think clearly, and I realized that the woman wasn't the problem. She didn't have a commitment to me, but he did.

I knew then that I had a decision to make. I could choose to think that it was my fault–that I should stay because this is as good as it's gonna get. I could choose to beat myself up, chastising myself for the way I looked, believing my old story that I wasn't pretty enough.

I could have gone into all the crazy stories that people tend to go into when they're feeling insecure, and there are thousands of them. Thank God, somehow in that moment, I knew I deserved better than this. For the first time in a relationship, I chose a different story: I get to be treated with respect, and I get to treat myself with respect.

I realized that I get to use discernment around who I trust. And I get to feel safe in relationships, but I didn't feel safe in this relationship anymore.

So, I left him.

For my sake, and the sake of the girls, I knew the breakup needed to be clean. I had to swiftly rip off the Band-Aid. So, I summoned all the strength I had to go against what felt natural, which was to stay in my comfort zone and to not ripple the waters, and I left.

Discovering My Worth

In that decision, I chose a bigger life for myself, and that is what I got.

I'm not saying that I walked away totally unscathed. I didn't. My insecurities still pop up sometimes today. I still work on trust, but I am constantly working on deciphering if the trust issues are mine, or if the other person has not proven themselves to be trustworthy.

I now have the tools that I get to apply to course correct and bring me back to a healthier way of thinking. In hard moments I ask myself:

- Is it true that I'm not safe in this relationship right now?

- Or is this an old insecurity and fear that's coming up, because I get to have a deeper level of breakthrough with it?

When I discovered that my fiancé had been unfaithful, I had a huge breakthrough, almost like getting hit by a spiritual Mack truck. It was a moment that catapulted me to my next level.

Because the pain was so deep, I knew I didn't want the universe to throw me anything bigger to test me in regards to knowing my worth. So I decided to hunker down and get the lesson of worthiness, that I deserve more and that I didn't need to settle.

I applied the very work that is now the One Thought Away Process to heal over the next few years, and it changed my life.

I came to understand that there were gaps in my life when I allowed myself to be treated poorly. During those times, I chose to believe the old stories from my past.

I had experiences as a child where I felt criticized, but it was my decision to believe what I was being told. It was my decision to accept it as my truth … or not.

When you're pointing outward and saying that someone did something to you or made you feel a certain way, it's time to take your power back. No one gets to make you feel a certain way. That's a choice that you, and only you, get to own.

That's right, you get to own your emotions and your mindset mastery. You get to own and understand your value and your worth. You have 100 percent capability of shifting what is happening that isn't serving you.

There might be moments when you wonder how you got back to where you started. You thought you already got that lesson. What happened?

Relax. It doesn't mean you're regressing. It doesn't mean you're going all the way back to square one and have to start all over. And it sure doesn't mean you didn't get the lesson the first time.

It just means you're now ready to take that lesson to a level deeper. You took that lesson to where you could back then, whether it was last year or 10 years ago, but you're different now. What if your results could be different now, as well? With mentorship, strategies, and a community that has your back, there is always the potential to benefit from the lessons that you're receiving.

Common Beliefs to Disrupt

You can have freedom from the beliefs that aren't working for you. My two big lessons in this lifetime relate to trust and self-worth. Maybe you'll recognize yourself in those, too, or in some of the beliefs listed below that I see often hold good people back...

- I'm not good enough.
- I didn't do enough.
- What if they leave me?
- When am I going to get picked?
- I have to do it all myself.

- What's wrong with me?
- I'm not lovable.
- I've been fooled.

Unfortunately, these examples just touch upon the many beliefs that go through our minds when we're hurt or disappointed. It is so easy to buy into these beliefs, but that will get us nowhere. The truth is, if we want to transform our lives, these beliefs must get disrupted.

Why are we inclined to fall back into these beliefs over and over? For one thing, some women have been socially conditioned to take on blame for things that are not theirs. And some cultures still see women as submissive, less than, or weaker than.

I think you can see how easy it is to believe these un-serving thoughts and how often we get subjected to them. If you've ever had a green underwear moment, your thinking may have taken you to the same place.

Lessons to Learn

The great thing is that we get to change those beliefs!

- I have always been good enough, even as I stretch into my next level of potential.
- I did the best I could and will continue to clean up where I didn't.
- I can trust the highest good is happening for me.
- There is a Divine Plan on my life, and I can trust it.
- I can trust myself and use appropriate discretion when trusting others.
- God did not make a mistake when he made me.
- I love myself unconditionally.
- Thank goodness I found out, now I get to create something better.

When I was on my journey of transformation, I was searching for answers, but didn't know where to find them. I didn't have a forward-thinking community. The people who had the answers and could help me weren't in my circle.

I've since discovered something incredible: As I continue to grow and change, my relationships and friendships change, as well. Don't be surprised if that happens to you, too. When that circle changes, it doesn't mean anything is wrong. It just means that you are having a higher level of awareness around what or who you're willing to allow, or not allow, into your space.

As I see people really step into their own, they start to form different types of friendships. This is a natural progression as you become the person you want to be and begin to have a different level of influence and impact on others.

That growth and transformation are natural, and Mary is a perfect example. Mary felt the changes in her relationships, as well as many other areas of her life. She was a client of mine; let me share more...

Mary's Story

"When I first started this journey, I was like a lost little lamb. I had tried to do so much on my own, and I just wasn't getting there. There were just so many pieces of my life that just felt a mess. I had a full-time job, but I worked part-time jobs to make ends meet at the time, as well. There were a lot of reasons I could have said I don't have time. I could have made excuses and lived in that story.

I was also in physical pain for 10 years. I felt pain every day of my life in some way, shape, or form. I'd had multiple cortisone shots in various parts of my body, including my elbows, knees, and hip. At one point, my ankles were the size of my thighs.

When I met Kerry, I literally jumped in with two feet, saying if I was going to do this, I was going to show up 110%, no matter what. That doesn't mean that it was always easy and that there weren't hard times and resistance, because, of course, that happens.

But I was dedicated, so I committed my time, my life, and my energy to doing this work to heal me, my soul, my heart, my physical self, my spiritual self, and every part of my being that needed and desired to be healed.

One thing that I do know so deeply from doing this work is that I felt like there was a part of me that was broken. Then there was another part of me that also felt that I didn't deserve to heal. But still, there was also that piece deep inside, and it was deep down, a little voice that said, "I deserve this. I do deserve to be whole."

As I did the work and I grew and transformed, that little voice got louder and stronger. I learned self-love is everything, and once you have that, you can do anything.

That's what One Thought Away does; it gives you self-love and belief in yourself. It doesn't mean I show up perfect. It doesn't mean I say all the right things and do all the right things, because I don't. And that's okay. I don't beat myself up over it. I have seen my growth. I'm never the victim anymore.

The biggest element of what cleaned up my physical pain was doing this emotional work and releasing trauma. Forgiving myself was the key to releasing my physical pain and my body beginning to heal. I've even gone on to do Ironman races, something I would have never been able to do before. Back then, there were days when just getting out of bed was physically hard."

The Mind-Body Connection and Why It Matters

Mary is proof that the mind-body connection is a very real thing. You can't separate the two and expect to heal. If you focus solely on your physical body to heal or improve your health, you're only working half the equation. The inner work is critical to sustainable transformation and sustainable results.

An unhealthy relationship with yourself will take a toll on your physical and emotional health. You are one thought away at all times—one thought away from accepting so much less than you should have, or one thought away from proclaiming that you deserve so much more.

You don't have to deal with someone else's toxicity. When you proclaim your own worth, you are able to purge those things from your life … and your bed.

CHAPTER 4

One Thought Away

THAT'S NOT MY UNDERWEAR!

When you're pointing outward and saying that someone did something to you, or made you feel a certain way, it's time to take your power back. No one gets to make you feel a certain way. That's a choice that you, and only you, get to own.

You can have freedom from the beliefs that aren't working for you.

PART 1

1 Common Belief To Disrupt: I'm not good enough.
Lesson To Learn: I have always been good enough, even as I stretch into my next level of potential.

2 Common Belief To Disrupt: I didn't do enough.
Lesson To Learn: I did the best I could and will continue to clean up where I didn't.

3 Common Belief To Disrupt: What if they leave me?
Lesson To Learn: I can trust the highest good is happening for me.

4 Common Belief To Disrupt: When am I going to get picked?
Lesson To Learn: There is a Divine Plan on my life and I can trust it.

One Thought Away

THAT'S NOT MY UNDERWEAR!

When you're pointing outward and saying that someone did something to you, or made you feel a certain way, it's time to take your power back. No one gets to make you feel a certain way. That's a choice that you, and only you, get to own.

You can have freedom from the beliefs that aren't working for you.

PART 2

5 Common Belief To Disrupt: I have to do it all myself.
Lesson To Learn: I can trust myself and use appropriate discretion when trusting others.

6 Common Belief To Disrupt: What's wrong with me?
Lesson To Learn: God did not make a mistake when he made me.

7 Common Belief To Disrupt: I'm not lovable.
Lesson To Learn: I love myself unconditionally.

8 Common Belief To Disrupt: I've been fooled.
Lesson To Learn: Thank goodness I found out, now I get to create something better.

#onethoughtaway | support@kerrytepedino.com | www.onethoughtawaybook.com

Chapter Five

I Can't Do That!

"I am connected to the eternal energy source, so I am not like a battery that gets used up," said Amma, the Hugging Saint, of her fast-paced schedule that many might claim was unrealistic, if not impossible, to maintain.

I have the strongest admiration for her, and her words have served as a reminder to me that I get to focus on what is possible, rather than a preconceived notion of what is impossible.

Amma's Story

Let me tell you about Amma.

Years ago, I traveled through India as a volunteer, assisting in the humanitarian efforts of Mata Amritanandamayi, a woman who has been recognized as a top spiritual leader of the twenty-first century. Otherwise known as Amma, or the Hugging Saint, she grew up a poor, uneducated village girl in the Kerala region of India. She later had so much impact that she was a keynote speaker at the Parliament of World Religion.

It was a rewarding, and difficult journey as a volunteer. During the two months I traveled with Amma, we made 23 stops across India, easily serving 100,000 people at one stop. People would wait up to 20 hours to receive a blessing, in the form of a hug, from Amma herself.

I have the strongest admiration for her, and her words have served as a reminder to me that I should focus on what is possible, rather than a preconceived notion of what is impossible.

After long bus drives from one event location to the next, and long hours of service, we would end our days sleeping on the hard concrete floors of the local school rooms. We pushed desks to the side to make room to lay our sleeping bags down. We then focused on creative ways to hang up our mosquito nets to protect ourselves from the relentless bugs.

That trip turned out to be a life-changing experience. I learned so much about the power of selfless service. I also learned so much about shifting one's mindset to know we can accomplish anything we set our mind to, if we want it badly enough.

Due to her childhood, Amma could have easily doubted herself, her capabilities, her impact, and her ability to fully and completely step into her power. Given her background, it would have been easy to fall into the common belief that she wasn't worthy of a role of influence.

Being a poor village girl in India, Amma could have believed she didn't deserve an education—at least, that's what her family told her on numerous occasions. At the young age of nine, she stopped going to school so she could help her ill mother take care of her siblings and the house.

As part of her chores, she'd gather scraps of food from neighbors, so she could feed her family's cows. It was during those door-to-door visits that Amma witnessed the extreme poverty and suffering that inspired her to help the people in need in her own community.

Amma was so compelled to help others that when she met people in need, she would bring them food and clothing from her own home, although she was often punished by her parents for doing so.

Not only did she give people food and clothing, she began to give them something more meaningful. Young Amma gave these families a warm embrace, bringing comfort to them in their time of need. It was this affection that earned her the nickname Amma, which means Mother.

Over the course of time, Amma developed a bigger vision for her life than that of a poor village girl. She was on a mission to make a difference not only in her community, but in her country and across the world.

How does a poor village girl become world renowned? Like so many who are impoverished, she could have felt hopeless, believing that her life would never expand beyond the scope of her village. She could have scrapped her vision, thinking it would be nothing short of impossible for her to go out into the world and make an impact on others.

But she didn't. She CHOSE a different future for herself. Thought by holy thought, she trusted in God to give her the next step to take and what to believe in.

To date, Amma has gifted her embrace to more than 37 million people, and her $6.25-million-dollar charity helps to support disabled people and malnourished pregnant women in India. And it's all because she refused to let anyone or anything hold her back.

It is so easy to buy into beliefs that keep us from living into our potential, influenced from our childhood circumstances. We can allow them to impact our thinking, in turn impacting our lives, or we can decide to turn them around. Turning them around starts with first an awareness of what they are, and then a thought to make it happen.

What beliefs do you have that are holding you back?

I wonder if you can resonate with any of these…

Common Beliefs to Disrupt

- It's impossible.
- There's not enough.
- It won't work for me.
- I don't have the background … the influence … the power.
- There's no way I can do that.
- These are the cards I've been dealt.
- I'm meant to suffer.
- I have nothing to give.

The good news is that you can go from "I can't" to "Darn right, I can!" if you choose to. Whatever seems impossible can be possible, if you allow yourself to believe it is.

In each obstacle, hardship, or limited belief, there are lessons that you can learn that will break the pattern that is holding you back.

Were you born in poverty? Have you been the victim of abuse, bullying, or discrimination? Perhaps you are working with cultural beliefs that held you back?

I challenge you to open your mind to a new possibility. What is the lesson you can learn from the hardship? And what do you want to do with it from here?

Amma was able to move beyond any limiting beliefs that could have held her back, and, in doing so, she became more influential than perhaps she'd ever thought possible. Like Gandhi and the Dalai Lama, she touched more lives across the globe than anyone could have imagined. She chose to break free from the stories that she was told and those she may have initially told herself.

Many people hold themselves back because of fear. There is the fear that even if they put in the effort, the time, the energy, or the resources that they'll still be stuck where they are.

For some, there's a fear that they'll never be able to change their old habits and end up right back where they started.

Perhaps it's a fear that they really don't have what it takes to make a difference. If it's not going to work, why even try? Some people are held back by procrastination. They put off any attempt to do something, because they either don't believe they can do it, or they're afraid that they'll be disappointed if they try.

What if we allowed this to be a defining moment and stopped letting fear drive our decisions?

Most people's brains are naturally wired to think about the worst-case scenario. This is largely due to the self-preservation thinking of our ancient ancestors, who didn't know what dangers might be lurking around them. For this reason, they took the worst-case, better be safe than sorry, route of thinking.

This tendency to lean toward the worst-case scenario has a name: catastrophizing. And it's quite common, especially among those between 18 and 35 years of age. This is when people are likely to be doing uncertain, risky things for the first time. Some examples are embarking on a new career, getting married, having children, or buying their first house.

It's all part of the subconscious mind at work, trying to protect us from getting hurt or making mistakes. But research also shows that those worst-case scenarios don't usually happen.

But yet, here we are, still buying into them, giving them the time they need to take seed and take over. It can monopolize the way we view the world and ourselves.

It's time to turn those fear-based beliefs into lessons that will lend themselves to a different scenario.

Lessons to Learn:

- Of course, it is possible!
- There's always enough.
- I can do anything I set my mind to.
- I always have what I need and more.
- I can figure anything out.
- Being born into a situation doesn't mean I have to stay there.
- God has bigger plans for me.
- I am abundant and love to give.

The choice is yours. You are one thought away from having the courage to move beyond your upbringing and your circumstances. The first step is to make the decision to go for it. Often, once we have made the leap, we understand that the hardest part was the jump itself, not what was waiting for us beyond the jump.

It only takes one step to begin to see a different result. With that one step, you begin to build momentum. One good result, however small it might be, will lead to another. Feeling good, you'll take the next step, then the next. Over time, those little steps add up, and looking back, you'll see just how far you've come.

Until you have a different thought that leads to a different action, you cannot expect different results. If you continue to have yesterday's thoughts and take yesterday's actions, you will get yesterday's results.

Initially, it might feel uncomfortable to have a different thought and action, but what's even more uncomfortable is staying stuck. Growth can be scratchy and itchy sometimes. Get past that feeling, knowing that every step you take will become more comfortable over time. And the new actions you're taking will be retraining your brain into creating different results.

Remember, your thoughts are influencing how you feel. How you think and feel are influencing the actions that you take. The consistent actions you take become your habits. Your habits create your results.

One thing leads to another ... and another ... and another, so this is a good time to ask yourself, "Where are my thoughts leading me?"

A Defining Moment

Beliefs that have been ingrained in us since childhood can be difficult to change. After all, we've held onto them our whole life. They have become our baseline and often we don't know anything different.

Once you can see these beliefs as an outdated belief system, you will have the opportunity to commit to shifting them. Only then can you forge ahead and create different beliefs that will guide you out of the past and into the present moment–in turn, creating an opportunity for an upleveled future.

I understand the fear that may come up to go to this level of honesty with yourself, to look at how you got to where you are today. But I believe there must also be another conversation going on inside of you saying that you can do and feel better–that you are worthy, and you deserve more.

So, let's pause and do an exercise to help you get in touch with the beliefs that aren't serving you and recognize them for what they are today.

It's time to take out a blank piece of paper and take a few minutes to write down every one of your wins over the past six months. Write down every success, no matter how small.

You lost five pounds? Great! Write it down.

You finished a project before the deadline? Write that down, too.

You opened a savings account? That's a win.

You took a class. Fantastic, add it to the list.

You ended a toxic relationship. Amen!

You get the idea. Once you're done writing down every one of your successes, put down your pen, close your eyes, put one hand on your heart and another on your belly. Take a few deep inhales and exhales.

Allow yourself to become present.

When you have quieted yourself, open your eyes and go back over your list, line by line and OWN each one of those wins. All of them, big and small.

Own each one of them with pride. Recognize what it took to create that result. Each one of these results happened because YOU thought certain thoughts and showed up in a certain way.

Allow yourself to realize that if you've been successful even once with something, you can be successful again.

How?

By applying the same way of THINKING and being to the breakthrough you want to create today. By applying a no-matter-what mindset and intentional actions to follow it.

By making a DECISION to give that goal you want everything you have got.

You shift your thinking and then you match those thoughts with your new way of BEING and look out! They'll take on a life of their own!

The purpose of this exercise is to show you that you have a *choice*. Your thoughts are not out of your control. They are a choice—*your* choice. And the actions you take because of those thoughts are your choice, as well.

This exercise, and the wins you wrote down, are the proof you need to abolish the story in your mind that says you don't have what it takes to create the life that you want.

That story is a lie. You know how I know that? Because you just created a list of wins that proves different. That story that you've been telling yourself that you "can't do it" is not true. Your list of successes tell a different story.

If you're still stuck in the past, you are experiencing what I call a disconnect. There's a disconnect between your beliefs and what you've actually already accomplished.

It's time to reconnect yourself with new beliefs that are aligned to the person you want to be today. Allow yourself to be that person now and become more loyal to that version of you than to any other version you have ever been.

A little action plan every day produces big results over time.

Make yourself a priority and give yourself time today to invest in creating a different life result TODAY and build your new life, one thought at a time.

Remember, a little action plan every day produces big results over time.

With consistency, you will naturally start to show up as that person who is successful. That person that creates wins. That person whose first thought is, "I can do this."

Let go of the baggage of the limiting beliefs that you've carried for far too long. You are just one thought away from reprogramming yourself to know that you can do hard things. You don't have to be stuck in mediocrity in any area of your life ever again.

With the right strategies and support you can become abundant, lose the weight, believe in yourself, become the one to find the one, create a legacy. Heal.

The ability is already inside of you. And if you've already created incredible results before, you can do it again. And you have your list of successes to prove it.

When you do create that next amazing result, add it to your *Success List*. It counts. Every success counts and when celebrated starts to reshape your belief system and ongoing results.

Let your *Success List* remind you of what you're capable of and what is possible. Let it give you the fuel and energy to move beyond your fear. As Albert Einstein taught us, everything is energy, which includes your emotions. That energy of fear can't be destroyed. It will transmute into something else. So, let's use it as fuel to shift us into a conversation of gratitude and possibility.

Your thoughts and feelings are energy, and they have the power to hold you back and sabotage you or catapult you into an entirely different life— your dream life.

Amma's thoughts took her far, far away from her poor village life.

What are the thoughts you have today about yourself and your life? Where are your thoughts taking you? You are the source of all the results you have in your life right now, and all the results you DON'T have in your life right now.

What are you thinking?

One Thought Away

I CAN'T DO THAT

It is so easy to buy into beliefs that keep us from living into our potential, often influenced from our childhood. What are the thoughts you have today about yourself and your life? What thoughts are moving you forward to the life you want? Celebrate those! And what are the thoughts that are holding you back?

Where are your thoughts taking you?

PART 1

1 Common Belief To Disrupt: It's impossible.
Lesson To Learn: Of course it is possible!

2 Common Belief To Disrupt: There's not enough.
Lesson To Learn: There's always enough.

3 Common Belief To Disrupt: It won't work for me.
Lesson To Learn: I can do anything I set my mind to.

4 Common Belief To Disrupt: I don't have the background ... the influence ... the power.
Lesson To Learn: I always have what I need and more.

One Thought Away

I CAN'T DO THAT

It is so easy to buy into beliefs that keep us from living into our potential, often influenced from our childhood. What are the thoughts you have today about yourself and your life? What thoughts are moving you forward to the life you want? Celebrate those! And what are the thoughts that are holding you back?

Where are your thoughts taking you?

PART 2

5 Common Belief To Disrupt: There's no way I can do that.
Lesson To Learn: I can figure anything out.

6 Common Belief To Disrupt: These are the cards I've been dealt.
Lesson To Learn: Being born into a situation doesn't mean I have to stay there.

7 Common Belief To Disrupt: I'm meant to suffer.
Lesson To Learn: God has bigger plans for me.

8 Common Belief To Disrupt: I have nothing to give.
Lesson To Learn: I am abundant and I love to give.

Chapter Six

Woman, Give Yourself a Voice!

"*I*f you don't let not knowing how it's done intimidate you, it's amazing what you can do. Failure is not the outcome. Failure is not trying."

A woman by the name of Sara Blakely spoke those words from experience. While you might not know who she is, if you're a woman, it's likely that you've heard of her company, Spanx.

The truth is, Spanx would have never been a household name if Sara Blakely hadn't been compelled to persist, speak up, and not let the naysayers stifle her dream.

Sara isn't alone. Women have long strived to be recognized for their entrepreneurial spirit and business acumen. However, for many, that has proved to be a struggle. In reality, they have the knowledge, the drive, and the leadership skills to be influential leaders, but yet they are often the last in line when it comes to climbing the proverbial corporate ladder.

Let's pause for a moment to make something clear. While I refer to women, it's important to note that this chapter is for the gentlemen out there, too. But I speak directly to our sisters here, because I feel there is a message that they get to hear, if they are open to it.

Why are there so few women seated at corporate boardroom tables?

According to WorldBank.org', females comprised less than 6.7 percent of board chairs globally in 2021, and only 25 percent of Fortune 500 board members were women.

Adding to that already low representation, it has been reported that Fortune 500 boardrooms are experiencing a significant loss of female leaders. They are walking away from their positions, feeling slighted that they didn't receive the project or promotion that they rightfully deserved.

In other words, their voices are not being heard. In some instances, they feel that their voices are stifled altogether.

Sara Blakely is the perfect example of a woman who rose above the stereotype and refused to keep her thoughts and her opinions to herself. Blakely was named in *Time* magazine's "Time 100" annual list of the 100 most influential people in the world. In 2014, she was listed as the 93rd most powerful woman in the world by *Forbes*.

Sara was the typical girl next door who left no stone unturned to bring her big dream into fruition. She sold fax machines, walking door to door in the hot Florida sun. In her role, and because she was a woman, she was required to wear pantyhose every day; however, she had a strong dislike for the way the seam across the toes looked in open-toed shoes.

In an attempt to find a solution, Sara cut the feet off her pantyhose, but that created a new problem—without closed toes, the pantyhose kept rolling up her legs. Yet, she liked the way the control top pantyhose made her body look firmer and the way they eliminated her panty lines. So Sara set out to create a product that would control without rolling.

Two years later, she introduced Spanx.

She drove to North Carolina, which is home to the majority of hosiery mills in America, and without a formal advertising or marketing campaign or staff, to present her idea. Every representative she approached turned her down.

She was a one-woman show, the founder and CEO, chief marketing officer, and only employee in her company. In addition, she had no experience at all.

When she went home, Sara was contacted by one mill operator, a man, who offered to lend support to her concept. While he didn't initially see the value in the product she'd invented, he had daughters who liked the idea and encouraged him to help it along.

That's when Sara realized that the hosiery industry was run by men ... people who weren't using the products. She realized then that she had to take her idea to the people who would use her product, and she personally marketed it to them in the stores where they shopped.

Without employees, she stood in stores by herself, using her voice to showcase her products, ending up with accounts in major fashion store chains, including Neiman Marcus. Single handedly, Sara catapulted her business forward and gained the attention and the approval of Oprah Winfrey and her massive audience.

She now is one of the few women who is invited into high level meetings, where she stands as an equal, does not hesitate to state her opinion, and is pioneering the way for other women to do the same.

In 2021, when the Blackstone Group acquired a majority interest in Spanx, Sara retained the position of Executive Chairwoman. At the time, her net worth was more than one billion dollars. To celebrate, she gave each of her employees a $10,000 bonus as a reward for their contribution to the company's success.

Sara Blakely had a dream, and it was a big one, at that. She was one female who encountered a male-dominant industry and was challenged with the difficulty of selling a product for females to people who knew nothing about them and wouldn't use them.

Sure, this can be intimidating, so much so that many people would feel like they'd hit a brick wall and give up. But instead of giving up, she decided to speak up. Without a team, she took her voice on the road and sold her products to women in the very places where they bought them.

This would have never happened if Sara, like so many others, had taken a different stance and let some common beliefs quell her dream.

Common Beliefs to Disrupt:

- What if I'm not chosen?
- What if I fail?
- What if my peers laugh at me?
- What if nobody cares?
- What if I get no support?
- What if I get negative feedback?
- What if I'm rejected?

These beliefs are the same as those of many females in C-suites and boardrooms across the country. They know they're alone or a part of the minority and fear that they won't be taken seriously. That fear pushes them into silence. By saying nothing, they believe they won't be subjected to criticism, rejection, or even ridicule by others.

Being silent is a double-edged sword. Sure, it can protect you from criticism and ridicule, but it also keeps your ideas and contributions under lock and key … where no one will know the value you can bring to your team, your company, or your organization.

Now, while this example is focused on females and their specific obstacles and challenges, it can also relate to other groups. A young adult might feel inferior to or not valued among a group of senior executives. Someone from a different culture or country might feel isolated or misunderstood.

When I was in the Peace Corps, even though I had studied Polish so I could communicate and make friends, my grasp of the language wasn't strong at all, leaving me unable to carry on deeper conversations and often misunderstood.

And anyone can feel like they're not being heard or appreciated because of who they are or what they express. This shows up on a daily basis for people at work, school, in homes, relationships, parenting and more.

Because you are here now, you are one thought away from finding your voice and expressing it in a way that people can hear you better. And sharing it with those who want to hear it and will benefit from hearing it.

By embracing the lessons within the challenges, we learn how to stand up and stand out (in a good way) and be recognized for our unique thoughts and ideas.

Lessons to Learn:

- I am the person who goes for it, no matter what!
- I am willing to do whatever it takes.
- I believe in me.
- I have value to give, but people won't know unless I share.
- I am resourceful and can find the support I need.
- Feedback is neutral, and I can choose what I want to do with it.
- Each rejection is one step closer to a yes.

Every perception or belief has a flip side that can be equally as powerful, and I might venture to say that it can be even more powerful. Negativity is a dream killer, but positivity is a dream maker. Positive thoughts are powerful motivators that give us the wherewithal to move forward and plow through the obstacles, real or imaginary, that are in front of us.

For example…

"What if they laugh at me?" gets to become…
"What if they love my idea?"

"What if they say no?" gets to become…
"Wouldn't it be incredible if they said yes?!"

"It'll never work. I shouldn't even try" gets to become…
"This really could work. I won't know until I try!"

"I'll never get the promotion, so why bother?" gets to become…
"If they don't know I'm interested, I won't get the job. I'm going to give it my best shot and see what happens."

Sara Blakely is a true American success story and a powerful example of creating a mindset that is based on "What if it DOES work out for me?"

The mother of four, she never gave up and never gave in to those who told her that they didn't see a market for her products. She never quit because others didn't have faith in her abilities due to her lack of experience. And she refused to bow down to those who were trusted to make decisions for a demographic that they weren't part of.

Sara was alone, and she was trying to make a deal on someone else's court … and it wasn't working. That's when she saw an opportunity. Even though she had no team or support system, she bypassed the manufacturing executives altogether and took her product straight to the stores and consumers she was marketing to.

And it worked!

Today, women across the world thank God that they have Spanx, which has become a staple in many women's wardrobes. And they are grateful for Sara Blakely showing them that they also have a voice and can use it.

Let's not forget that being a woman in a male-dominated industry isn't the only situation when people can learn to use their voice. A male could feel intimidated or undervalued in a female-dominated industry. Any minority that is underrepresented in a boardroom might feel uncomfortable speaking up. Perhaps they don't want to call attention to themselves or believe (whether or not it is validated) that they are looked upon differently than their peers.

And how about those who were raised in a different culture, one where it is considered rude to speak up without being asked for their opinion? Or a culture where it is taught that it is inappropriate to disagree with superiors or elders?

As you can see, there are so many reasons why people, both male and female, young and senior, might not feel that their voice is welcome.

We just discussed Sara Blakely, a female selling a product for females in a male-dominated industry, but it's not specific only to corporations. How about academia, where it might be unusual to have a female professor in programs that are traditionally taught by males? Or vice versa, a male professor in programs that are traditionally pursued by females?

Situations such as these are not disputable, and they are being vigorously addressed in today's STEM (science, technology, engineering, math) training to males and females alike. And that's a good thing, because when everyone feels welcome and comfortable in their industry, their position, and their environment, they are more inclined to speak up, speak out, provide feedback, and share their thoughts and unique ideas.

In other words, they are being taught at a young age to dispel common myths.

Now, let's apply this to you. Was there a time, at work or in your personal life, when you held back your thoughts, opinions, or ideas for fear of what other people might think?

How did that impact the life you're living right now?

Is it possible that if you had spoken up, you would be in a different place in your career? Would you have more income? Or more influence?

Do you often wonder "what if?"

- What if I had spoken up and taken credit for my idea?
- What if I had applied for that promotion?
- What if I had the confidence to state all of my qualifications and strengths?
- What if I had the nerve to tell someone about my idea and they actually liked it?
- What if I had been the person that goes for it?
- How would my life and my world be different today?

And here's the big question:

What if I hadn't silenced my dreams by silencing my voice?

Imagine what would or could have happened if you had applied for that promotion, spoken up, shared an idea, or gone all out for something you really wanted. If you had done any of those things differently and knew what the outcomes would be, do you think you would have been more willing to take those risks?

You might be surprised to discover that the different outcome you experienced far outweighs your reluctance to express yourself and be assertive. If the results were amazing, do you think you would finally recognize that you have value and worth that shouldn't be silenced?

You do have value, and you deserve to be heard. There are people who will benefit from your ideas and contributions. Speak up for them. Speak up for yourself. Speak up!

You are not walking this walk alone—Sara and so many others have paved the way for you. Follow their lead by tightening your thoughts, finding your voice and see where it can take you.

CHAPTER 6
One Thought Away
WOMAN, GIVE YOURSELF A VOICE!

Being silent is a double-edged sword. Sure, it can protect you from criticism, but it also keeps your ideas and contributions under lock and key. If your voice is not heard, no one will know the value you can bring to those you care about, your team, company, or the world.

You do have value, and you deserve to be heard. There are people who will benefit from your ideas and contributions. Speak up!

PART 1

1 Common Belief To Disrupt: What if I'm not chosen?
Lesson To Learn: I am the person who goes for it, no matter what!

2 Common Belief To Disrupt: What if I fail?
Lesson To Learn: I am willing to do whatever it takes.

3 Common Belief To Disrupt: What if my peers laugh at me?
Lesson To Learn: I believe in me.

4 Common Belief To Disrupt: What if nobody cares?
Lesson To Learn: I have value to give, but people won't know unless I share.

One Thought Away

WOMAN, GIVE YOURSELF A VOICE!

Being silent is a double-edged sword. Sure, it can protect you from criticism, but it also keeps your ideas and contributions under lock and key. If your voice is not heard, no one will know the value you can bring to those you care about, your team, company, or the world.

You do have value, and you deserve to be heard. There are people who will benefit from your ideas and contributions. Speak up!

PART 2

5 Common Belief To Disrupt: What if I get no support?
Lesson To Learn: I am resourceful and can find the support I need.

6 Common Belief To Disrupt: What if I get negative feedback?
Lesson To Learn: Feedback is neutral and I can choose what I want to do with it.

7 Common Belief To Disrupt: What if I'm rejected?
Lesson To Learn: Each rejection is one step closer to a yes.

#onethoughtaway | support@kerrytepedino.com | www.onethoughtawaybook.com

Chapter Seven

Am I Enough?

"Careers and opportunities like this have never happened for women in my family."

"What do you mean?"

"Well, I am the first person in my family to not only go to college, but to get a master's degree–not to mention to become an educator myself. In my family, it is unheard of."

"You should be proud of yourself, Rose. You made it happen."

Rose wiped away a tear, thinking of the long road it had been to get herself to where she was today. "Sometimes I just can't believe that this is my life. I am so grateful I never gave up."

Rose is not only an African American woman who has made a mark for herself as an educator, but she is someone who faced all odds of building a life for herself that was not supposed to be possible for her in the first place.

Rose faced a difficult childhood where she was constantly told she wasn't good enough. She was berated for not living up to standards, and it felt as if she had life stacked up against her. Throughout all her challenges, she still climbed the professional ladder and used personal development as her main tool as she forged ahead.

She spent time and energy honing her mindset mastery and emotional mastery skills, so that no matter what life threw at her, it didn't derail her from her vision and dream.

She is an incredible example of how, when we don't take no for an answer and when we refuse to believe we must stay in the confines others want to put on us, we can defy all odds and pioneer another path, even on the path less taken.

So many women feel as if they must be defined by their childhoods or hold themselves back from having a voice in the workforce. They miss incredible opportunities for success, achievement, growth, financial abundance, and recognition.

Rose's story is an incredible one of grit, resilience, faith, and hope that has inspired the heck out of me to buckle down and overcome all obstacles.

For Rose, it started when she was sent to her grandmother, who raised her. Both parents needing to work, she didn't have the attention, acknowledgement, or the love from her parents she hungered for.

She believed she must have done something wrong for them to leave her, she wasn't good enough, and if she had been better, perhaps they would have stayed.

She has a lot of painful memories and ideas about her childhood that she carried with her throughout her life, until she did the One Thought Away Process.

Still, with what might be viewed by some as a childhood disadvantage, Rose succeeded above and beyond what most people would imagine.

She chose to be a woman who worked hard to believe in herself, resulting in her having a massive impact and influence on her students and those in her life. That all came about because of her willingness to have a vision and develop a no-matter-what mindset to attain it.

How did Rose overcome the circumstances of her youth? It started with a thought. She decided it was important to her. It was worth whatever it took for her to achieve her vision for her life.

If your vision is important to you, you'll do whatever it takes, too, despite your perceived disadvantages or limitations.

That's what Rose did. She became an educator who made a mark on the world. And she went on to give birth to two of her own babies and became the mother that she never had the opportunity to experience.

And she did it admirably.

Sure, it was a challenge for her. Never having had her own parents in her life, she didn't know how to be one herself. But she refused to allow herself to get stuck and become another statistic. She refused to carry on the family lineage of no one going to college, or having a career they chose for themselves, all the while being an attentive and loving mom.

If Rose can achieve her dreams, so can you. Start by disrupting the beliefs that are holding you back from making your mark on the world.

Common Beliefs to Disrupt:

- I can't.
- It's not my place.
- Life ripped me off.
- I am always the underdog.
- This isn't the life I was meant to live.
- I don't have the tools, the people, the support that it takes.
- Struggle is normal.

I'm wondering... are there people around you who say, "You can't dream that big," "Who do you think you are?" "What makes you think you deserve that?"

Or how about this often overused excuse from naysayers, "Nobody in the history of our family has ever gone that far in life, it's not who we are."

If you've heard (or told yourself) some of those lines, you're not alone. It's a common theme among the stories and examples I've shared with you in this book. From Barack Obama finally believing in himself and owning his power by taking pride in himself and his heritage, to Amma, the poor girl from the fishing village who changes the life of hundreds of thousands of people every year.

Truth or Fiction?

There are countless examples of people who overcame their circumstances, their youth, their socioeconomic conditions, and their naysayers … including the naysayer within.

And you can, too.

Tiny seeds get planted in our minds when we are young. They are the formation of what we will grow into, what we're capable of, and who we will become.

But sometimes we give those seeds too much attention and focus. We fertilize the rotten ones, and they grow like weeds. They pop up whenever we consider a different outcome. The sunshine gets blocked, and our futures look anything but bright. These weeds, or limitations, put screeching halts on who we can become.

They might not have any truth to them whatsoever, but we believe them.

You can pull up those weeds and keep the rotten seeds from multiplying and taking over. You can absolutely break out of all the confines that are restricting you. Cut the chains off your ankles and wrists that say you have to be a certain way or that you were born into a destiny you cannot escape.

Your birth, upbringing, family's history, and the perceived disadvantages that you were born into do have an impact and an influence on you, but they do not have to dictate who you are now and moving forward.

If you focus on your personal development and experience more success because of it ... with your health, relationships, money, career, education, weight, confidence ... you'll realize that you can choose to be unstoppable.

Lessons to Learn:

- I will do whatever it takes.
- I deserve to be here.
- I can make a better life for myself starting now.
- My past circumstances do not dictate my future successes.
- I am made for more!
- I am bigger than my circumstances.
- Life is meant to be fun and easy.

For every thought that is holding you back from what you want and truly deserve in this life, there is a lesson that you need to learn in order to dispel that thought and replace it with one that jump starts your motivation, mind, and body into action.

What is the one thought that will remove the boundaries, perceived or otherwise, that are holding you back?

Making Your Dream a Reality

If there's a dream in your heart, there's a reason why you have that dream. Believe that with a conviction made of steel. Make a decision to believe that this gets to be your truth.

Whatever is in your heart is there because something in the universe is trying to tell you that it is possible. And something inside of you is daring to believe that is true.

Wherever you are in your life today, whether it's at rock bottom or whether your life is really going well, know that you can always level up again. There is nothing in the book of life that says you are where you are and that's where you need to stay.

You have a calling on your life. A Divine Plan is there for you. You're made for more. You're made to be more than a doormat. You're made to be more than the hurt victim of infidelity. You're made for more than believing that your body can't heal or that you will always be poor.

God does not make mistakes. And you are not a mistake.

You can choose to be the person you want to be. The only person who can stop you from becoming that person is yourself–or more accurately put, your thoughts.

The first step to becoming that person is to believe in yourself. Believe in what you're capable of and what's possible for you. Believe in your dreams.

The second step is to identify the areas and experiences in your life that might be standing between you and your dreams.

I like to use a journal for this. I will feed you questions, and as I do, I want you to stop reading and write down your answers.

Let's get started…

1. What is the #1 breakthrough you want this year?

2. Why is it important to you?

3. What has been stopping you from getting that result, up until this point?

4. What payoff are you getting from holding yourself back? Do you get to look good, play safe, or be right?

5. What is it costing you in your life to not just go for it?

Become a detective and investigate where your thoughts and beliefs stem from. Whether you discover that you lack faith in yourself or have underlying fears, your answers will reveal what you get to address. You will start to get clues on the stories you get to dispel and the lessons you get to learn in order to overcome them.

Think of it this way–you don't have anything to lose. You do have everything to gain.

Silencing the negativity of the mind is empowering.

We all have stories that work overtime to keep us from stepping out of our comfort zone. But when we recognize them as stories that don't need to hold our truth any longer, we find strength to counter them and create new results.

Silencing the negativity of the mind is empowering. It's helped me tremendously. Whenever I hear a negative story popping into my mind, I know it's time to course correct. Creating a pattern interrupt can help you break the normal pattern of the old story.

For example, when I recognize that I'm feeling low, I get up and dance. I don't care if it doesn't make me feel good right away, because I know it will eventually, especially if I am dancing silly with my kids. I know that by dancing, I'm doing something other than reinforcing those thoughts that don't serve me, as well as moving the stuck energy out.

Dancing gives me power over my doubts. It gives me power over my thoughts.

Find Your Power

What will give you power over your thoughts? You can have a power word, a word that will create an internal shift away from the limiting thoughts. For instance, if you catch yourself stinking thinking, you can energetically say out loud your power word to change your thinking.

SHIFT!

TRANSFORM!

PIVOT!

ALIGN!

Whatever word you train your mind with can take you out of your funk and bring you back to a positive present. Align yourself back to the fact that you are good enough, you are worthy, you are capable, and you've got this!

With that new thought comes the opportunity to make another decision. A different decision that will bring you closer to your dream life, rather than keeping it at bay.

Your thoughts influence your actions. Your actions impact your results.

Shift your thoughts into the direction that you want to be going ... not the direction where you've been.

Give yourself permission to be happy, regardless of what your past trauma was. Even if you've been violated or abused, lied to or cheated on, or perhaps you did things to yourself you are not proud of. Give yourself permission to be happy in this present moment and clean up what needs to be cleaned up.

You deserve it.

Just because you've been unhappy in the past, that doesn't mean that you have to continue to be unhappy. There's no contractual lifetime obligation to continue to suffer. You get to choose what to do and how to feel in the present moment.

Don't forget, too, that sometimes it is our traumas that feed our success. In some ways, they can catapult us to the next level because the access point to raw emotions and motivation is so real.

Rose is a perfect example. Nothing can hold her back from achieving success or wanting to become a loving mother herself.

Instead, she used the trauma from her childhood to overcome her challenges. Her parents leaving her fueled her desire to experience motherhood and be the best mom she could possibly be.

Like Rose, you might have been born into your circumstances, but that doesn't mean you have to stay there. It doesn't matter what side of the fence you were born on, you can always move.

You are enough, despite your traumas.

And that is one thought I invite you to hold onto.

One Thought Away

AM I ENOUGH?

So many women hold themselves back from having a voice, missing incredible opportunities for success, achievement, growth, financial abundance, and recognition. You can choose to be the person you want to be in every aspect of your life. The only person who can stop you from becoming that person is yourself. Or more accurately put, your thoughts.

Be unavailable to letting your thoughts hold you back.
It's time to turn them around!

PART 1

1 Common Belief To Disrupt: I can't.
Lesson To Learn: I will do whatever it takes.

2 Common Belief To Disrupt: It's not my place.
Lesson To Learn: I deserve to be here.

3 Common Belief To Disrupt: Life ripped me off.
Lesson To Learn: I can make a better life for myself starting now.

4 Common Belief To Disrupt: I am always the underdog.
Lesson To Learn: My past circumstances do not dictate my future successes.

CHAPTER 7

One Thought Away

AM I ENOUGH?

So many women hold themselves back from having a voice, missing incredible opportunities for success, achievement, growth, financial abundance, and recognition. You can choose to be the person you want to be in every aspect of your life. The only person who can stop you from becoming that person is yourself. Or more accurately put, your thoughts.

**Be unavailable to letting your thoughts hold you back.
It's time to turn them around!**

PART 2

5 Common Belief To Disrupt: This isn't the life I was meant to live.
Lesson To Learn: I am made for more!

6 Common Belief To Disrupt: I don't have the tools, the people, the support that it takes.
Lesson To Learn: I am bigger than my circumstances.

7 Common Belief To Disrupt: Struggle is normal.
Lesson To Learn: Life is meant to be fun and easy.

Chapter Eight

Perhaps I Should Play It Safe?

"*I* did it *again*! Why can't I stop this crazy cycle?"

That was the first thought I had after I slapped my alarm clock, hoping to give myself a few more minutes of sleep. That was before remembering that I had meetings I had to get up and be ready for.

Groggy, my feet hit the floor. Like many days before, I instantly realized that I felt terrible. I felt bloated and tired. My unhealthy habits and lifestyle were punishing me. I was a glutton for punishment and had broken trust with myself once again.

I should have taken care of myself the night before. I should have eaten a healthy dinner and gone to bed at a decent hour. I had been tired after a long day at work, but instead of taking care of myself and getting some much-needed rest, I chose to repeatedly overindulge in snacks, late into the night, to refuel my energy levels.

That obviously backfired. The next morning, I felt worse than I had before I'd gone to bed.

Why wasn't I taking care of myself and continuing this crazy pattern of binge eating? It occurred to me that maybe I was too far gone to turn things around … maybe I should just give up and let this food addiction win.

I even thought I should accept my life for what it was and play it safe and stay small. With low expectations, there would be less chance that I'd disappoint myself yet again. I was tired of reliving the frustration I had with myself for not loving myself and having the self-worth to give myself the basic care that I needed to survive.

For the umpteenth time, I asked myself, "What's the point of trying to break the cycle and trying to get better if it's not working for me?"

My 50-pound weight gain was the result of years of an eating disorder, which was a symptom of a lack of self-love, low self-esteem, not believing in myself and feeling as if I could never get "it" right.

"It" refers to the relationship, the project at work, the perfect day of eating and exercising, or whatever else was in front of me that day that had me feeling not good enough.

I spent so much time and energy on trying to be someone I wasn't, because I wasn't satisfied with who I was. To me, that person was not enough. My eating disorder was my way of dealing with my feelings of mediocrity and attempting to protect myself from feeling let down.

There was a time when my eating disorder controlled my life, and while I've claimed victory over it, there are still times when I'm reminded of its impact.

Not too long ago, I opened my fridge to look for something healthy to eat for lunch. As my eyes scanned the shelves for my options, they came to rest on a big chocolate bar that we'd bought to make s'mores while on a camping trip.

"Yum!," I would have said years before. Like I'd found a hidden treasure, I'd then grab it without a second thought and devour the whole thing, all the while telling myself I would have just a bite.

This time, though, I knew I wanted healthier alternatives, something that would keep me energized and focused. Instead of reaching in and grabbing that chocolate because it was there, I just noticed it … nothing more.

"I don't even want that right now," I thought.

I wasn't tempted at all. I didn't crave it and didn't even care that it was there. That's when I once again realized how much things had changed. Things were so different than how they used to be, and I was so grateful.

"I am unavailable to having an eating disorder again. I'm unavailable for feeling bad in my own body. I'm unavailable to betray myself ever again."

In the past, I would have been thinking of that chocolate bar in the fridge. I would have obsessed about it, even if I'd walked away from the fridge and gone to a totally different room. I wouldn't have been able to get my mind off that chocolate until I had devoured every bit of it, making excuses to justify having just one bite.

Hmmm, maybe I'll just go grab a small piece, what's the big deal?

I wouldn't have been able to get much else done if there was a chocolate bar in the fridge … if it was there, I had to have it, because that was where my mind was. I had an unhealthy obsession with food. As a result, I was stuck in a diet mentality.

It was a cycle that I felt I couldn't break, even if I wanted to. I didn't believe it was possible. If there was something enticing in the fridge, I had to have some. It would call to me like the haunted voice of temptation, and it would continue to call to me until I finally answered.

I knew I was hooked, and at times I resigned myself to the fact that there was nothing I could do about it. It was a craving I couldn't control, and even if there was a tiny possibility that I could conjure up the willpower to walk away and forget about what was calling my name, it didn't work for long.

What I didn't know was that I was telling myself a lie, it was never about willpower. It was about how I was *thinking*.

My belief system is totally different today. Every day, I affirm my self-love and worth.

"I enjoy respecting myself and my body. I am worthy of feeling great. I deserve to have the life I've always wanted."

Most of all, I realized that I no longer thought of the transformational changes that I'd made as work. No longer were they hard … they were simply my normal way of life.

And with that thought, I knew I would never again play it small. I had learned to conquer the old thoughts and beliefs that had held me back for far too long, and I was unavailable to entertain them ever again.

Common Beliefs to Disrupt:

- What's the point?
- Why can't I just be normal?
- The damage is already done.
- I'll do better tomorrow (you know, the day that never comes!).
- I can't stop; it's too hard.
- Nothing else works out the way I want.
- It's been a pattern for so long, I can't change it.
- I just can't.

Breaking the eating disorder was one of the hardest things I have ever done. I used to turn to food for comfort and solace. When everything and everyone, including myself, let me down, food never let me down. Not once. It was a one-size-fits-all treatment for anything that ailed me.

"Hey, Kerry, feeling left out and lonely? Here's a cookie."

"Upset that the project wasn't up to par? That's too bad. Here, you deserve a candy bar."

"Did someone hurt your feelings? A bowl of ice cream always helps."

Food, especially sugar-laden food, made me feel better. It soothed me, and over the years, I got into the habit of turning to it without even thinking about it.

Maybe you can relate. Do you have an unhealthy relationship with food? Caffeine? Anything? If so, you know the type of control it can have over you and how much you count on it to get you through a rough patch.

When I hit bottom that day on the bathroom floor, I knew I had to make drastic changes. Food was my fix, my band aid, and removing it as my crutch would force me to face what I was feeling. I was terrified.

Thank God, that day a new thought dropped into my mind at that moment…

"I *must* do something different."

That thought pushed me forward through many tough times as I healed. I learned that if you continue this work, the vices lose their power over you and you become stronger.

Today, I know I am strong enough to open the fridge and see a chocolate bar and walk away from it. I know that I can have one piece of a chocolate bar without having to consume the whole thing.

Chocolate no longer controls my thoughts. I control my thoughts.

What is the change that you know you need to make to move yourself forward, but you have been too scared to do it?

What is that costing you in your life? Your self-esteem? Your confidence? Your health? A promotion?

Now that you can see the negative impact this has had on your life, are you ready to make a change?

If so, you are just one thought away from the change you want to see. But you have to do the work and sometimes that can feel hard.

Nobody said it was going to be easy. In the moment, the easiest thing will feel like to stay in the cycle. That is taking you off course to the life you really want though. If you really want a transformed life, at some point you must change what you are thinking and the actions you are taking.

Otherwise, you're turning your back on the life you could have, swapping it for a life that's less than you deserve.

Are there risks involved when you attempt to conquer something that you've lived with for so long, whether it's food, pills, alcohol, or another vice or defense mechanism? Perhaps.

Maybe you'll struggle. Maybe it will expose what you consider a weakness. Maybe you'll doubt your strength or ability to change, and playing it safe right there where you are sounds a whole lot easier than facing the hard work to transform your life.

But I guarantee that it's not better or easier in the long run!

I was consumed by eating. It gave me the comfort that I longed for but didn't have in my life. Unfortunately, it also kept me from finding the type of comfort and affection I desperately wanted.

I'm here to tell you that you can overcome what you consider your struggle and break out of that comfort zone, which isn't really comfortable at all.

At some point in my life, I *thought* eating filled a void in my life. And when I became dependent on it to the point that eating became self-destructive, I *thought* it was beyond my control and that there was nothing I could do about it. I *thought* I absolutely needed emotional eating to get by.

That's a lot of thoughts!

My saving grace was having one more thought. What if my emotional eating was actually making things worse? Now, there's a thought.

What if my self-created vice was treating the symptoms, but not the cause? Now, that's a bigger thought.

What if I was worthy and had the strength, one thought at a time, to break this unhealthy cycle and create a healthier one?

What a thought!

Those were the thoughts that helped me get through the initial cravings that satisfied my emotions. I realized that neither eating nor other people were responsible for the way I viewed myself and the life I'd created.

And with each day that I made a healthier decision around eating, I learned something remarkable. Not only was I learning to enjoy healthy foods, but when I would indulge in something that I would have once considered unhealthy, I was surprised that it didn't have the same effect it once had on me. It didn't taste quite as good. It didn't make me feel better. I no longer needed it for a quick hit of relief.

And that was a life-changing thought.

They say a smile is a frown turned upside down. What if I told you that you could flip your thoughts in much the same way to create an opposite result? I did. It took a series of thoughts, one after another, to get me on track and keep me going.

You can flip your thoughts to get the results you want, too. Some people call it willpower, but I know that our thoughts are actually where our superpowers lie. Through the power of your thoughts, you can find the strength to break through your self-perceived barriers and put the brakes on your dependance of whatever vice is holding you back.

Lessons to Learn:

- Keep going! Growth is just outside my comfort zone.
- I am fine. Everyone has challenges.
- I can turn this around.
- I will take a positive action forward now!
- I can do hard things!
- I am willing to trust the process.
- I can transform my life one thought at a time.
- I can do anything!

What seems safe is actually what is holding you back.

Big results will demand you get into big action. Luckily, big action can start with a baby step.

It took work to break my eating disorder, and it wasn't always easy. I wondered what would become of me if I did the work and nothing changed. But it did, and it can change for you, too.

> Big results will demand you get into big action. Luckily, big action can start with a baby step.

I'm living proof that when I finally changed my thoughts, I was able to break my unhealthy eating habits. A huge weight was lifted off my shoulders. Gone were the guilt, shame, excuses.

When I escaped from my self-imposed prison, I was able to seek what I really wanted in life. The very things that had caused me to turn to emotional eating in the first place, were the things I wanted the most ... connection, love, acceptance, confidence, calm, freedom.

I now know that I no longer want to play it safe, because I want to play my life full out. I want to do things I never thought possible.

Now I know I am capable of breaking negative cycles. That doesn't mean it is always easy, but I have a roadmap. And I can reach for the stars and live the life of my dreams.

CHAPTER 8
One Thought Away
PERHAPS I SHOULD PLAY IT SAFE

What is the change needed to move yourself forward, but you have been too scared to do it? What is that costing you in your life? Are you willing to make a change?

**Big results will demand you get into big action.
Luckily, big action can start with a baby step.**

PART 1

1 Common Belief To Disrupt: What's the point?
Lesson To Learn: Growth is just outside my comfort zone.

2 Common Belief To Disrupt: Why can't I just be normal?
Lesson To Learn: I am fine. Everyone has challenges.

3 Common Belief To Disrupt: The damage is already done.
Lesson To Learn: I can turn this around.

4 Common Belief To Disrupt: I'll do better tomorrow (you know, the day that never comes!).
Lesson To Learn: I will take a positive action forward now!

One Thought Away

PERHAPS I SHOULD PLAY IT SAFE

What is the change needed to move yourself forward, but you have been too scared to do it? What is that costing you in your life? Are you willing to make a change?

**Big results will demand you get into big action.
Luckily, big action can start with a baby step.**

PART 2

5 Common Belief To Disrupt: I can't stop; it's too hard.
Lesson To Learn: I can do hard things!

6 Common Belief To Disrupt: Nothing ever works out the way I want.
Lesson To Learn: I am willing to trust the process.

7 Common Belief To Disrupt: It's been a pattern for so long, I can't change it.
Lesson To Learn: I can transform my life, one thought at a time.

8 Common Belief To Disrupt: I just can't.
Lesson To Learn: I can do anything!

Chapter Nine

Can't is Not in My Vocabulary

"Can't is *not* in our vocabulary!"

My stepfather spoke those words with so much conviction that it compelled the people around him to act, even when they had already insisted that what he wanted couldn't be done.

My stepdad has been my dad since I was three. He was super involved, quick to volunteer to be my softball coach and field trip chaperone when I was growing up. His military background made him strict as heck, but he was also fun, gladly letting a heap of kids pile up in his station wagon.

One night, as an adult years later, I was eating dinner when the phone rang. Seeing it was my parents, I picked up, happy to catch up on how they were doing. I had no idea that my world was about to come crashing down.

It was the call you pray you'll never get.

Dad was sick. Really sick. He had cancer. I felt hot, flushed, sick to my stomach. This can't be happening.

Thankfully, he triumphed, but four years later, the cancer returned with a vengeance. We knew it was going to be a much harder road this time.

I didn't want to take a moment for granted. I wanted to make sure we spent quality time together and had the conversations that were important to have with him.

One weekend, I really wanted to see him, so I threw a pair of jeans and a couple pairs of yoga pants into an overnight bag and headed out the door, just enough to get me through the weekend. I drove from San Diego to Sacramento, planning to stay a few days.

When I arrived, I swung open the front door, excited to be there and looking forward to the weekend together.

"Hi! I'm here!" I called out, checking out the kitchen but finding no one there.

"Mom, Dad ... I'm here!" I said loudly as I walked the long hallway down to the master bedroom.

I walked in and froze in my tracks, shocked at what I saw. I tried to act nonchalant as I choked back tears, witnessing how much his health had deteriorated since I'd last seen him.

I didn't get it. I didn't get how bad the situation had become. That first night showed me that things were not good, and the level of stress and effort on my mom to be his caregiver was big. Yet, she didn't complain. She loved him and was happy to do it.

Realizing the extent of the situation, I decided to stay. A couple days turned into weeks. Weeks turned into months. I thank God that I was able to work from their guest room and didn't need to return home right away.

There came a point in his battle that his body was retaining fluid. It was unbelievable how swollen and stretched his body became. Even worse, he was in a lot of pain.

On a Friday afternoon, he asked my mom to call the nurse to request a procedure. The procedure would drain the fluid from his body to give him some relief.

The nurse did not bring good news…

"I'm sorry, we don't book that procedure on a weekend. We will increase his medication for the weekend to give him some relief and look at booking it Monday morning."

Saturday morning came and the increased medication didn't help at all.

"Sheila, I really need that procedure. We need to call the nurse."

"Scott, don't you remember the nurse said we can't get the procedure on a weekend?"

"Can't is not in our vocabulary."

My mom, being the team player and loving wife that she is, looked at him and said, "You know what? You're right."

She got back on the phone with new determination and enrolled the nurse to call her director to do a house visit with my dad that very afternoon. As soon as he saw my dad, he put the order in for him to have the procedure that day.

After removing liters of fluid, my dad felt so much better. When he came home from the hospital at 2am, he began to take the ornaments off the Christmas tree.

"What are you doing, Scott?"

"I want to help, so you don't have to do it by yourself later."

While the procedure didn't last, it gave my dad some much-needed relief in the moment. My dad did succumb to his illness, passing just a couple weeks later. Our hearts were broken, but we celebrated his life just the way he planned for us to, with an incredible luau with friends and family.

My dad taught me many lessons, but "Can't is not in our vocabulary" was one of the most powerful. It made a huge impact on the way that I think and what I believe I am capable of.

I learned that if we have the right mindset and stretch ourselves out of our comfort zone, there is always a solution. It's about getting the right strategies, finding the necessary support, and surrounding ourselves with people who also believe anything is possible.

Taking His Words to Heart

My dad's beliefs rubbed off on me. In fact, they had a lifelong effect on me, ultimately changing my life and my family.

"Can't is not in our vocabulary" influenced me to have my first child on my own. I was 41 years old and single. The number one IVF doctor in San Diego had told me when I was 39 that I would never have children. The prospect of being childless devastated me.

One night, I went out for dinner with a friend, and we ran into another friend and asked her to join us. She asked how everything was going.

I immediately dove into my same story…

"I've been dating, but still haven't found anyone special. I still don't have kids, but I'm doing everything I can, and it's just not working out," I complained.

"No, you're not," she countered.

"What?"

"If you were doing everything you could to get pregnant, you'd exhaust every option," she stated boldly.

I couldn't believe she actually said that to me. I felt like she slapped me in the face. My initial reaction was anger.

Who does she think she is talking to me that way? What does she know? My mind raced.

Luckily, I'd done enough personal development work that I quickly turned that around. I knew in my heart that she was right. If I really wanted that result in my life, I would do whatever it took to make it happen.

This correlated with the first Father's Day after my stepfather passed away. I felt terribly alone when I went to visit him at the cemetery. It was dusk, and I was sitting on a bench near where he was laid to rest, pouring all of my emotions into my red leather-bound journal...

Forget fear! Nobody is going to tell me what I can and cannot do with my body. I'm taking back control!

It was like a switch flipped. The energy was so strong that it stayed with me until the next morning. I declared to myself that I was going for this– I was going to do whatever it took to be a mom.

I called a sperm clinic and made an appointment for the very next day. They gave me my instructions and access to their donor bank, so I could do my research.

The very next morning my basal temperature was exactly where it needed to be for a pregnancy. While I'd been taking my temps for quite some time, it had never been this perfect.

I instantly knew that God was on my side. He had His hands all over this.

Within a couple weeks, I discovered I was pregnant after years of being told it would never happen for me.

The last really important conversation I had with my stepdad was to have him help me name my future child. I wanted him to be a part of it, since I knew he would not be physically here for the occasion.

One night, his hospice nurse had asked him, "What is the first thing you noticed about your spouse?"

"Her grace," he immediately replied.

So, my first son became Grayson, my first true love and a boy filled with so much love and grace. Grayson Scott, named after my stepdad and a miracle baby born on his birthday!

This mindset also influenced me to have my twins, Chloe and Phoenix, through IVF at 48 years of age. I was committed to my dream of having a big family, no matter what the doctors and statistics were telling me.

Just as my stepfather could have chosen to accept the fact that a medical procedure couldn't be done, I could've accepted the likelihood that I would never become a mother or experienced the joys of having children.

I would have missed out on my three wonderful kids if I had resigned myself to the "fact" that motherhood "can't" happen for me.

Today, I am fortunate to have the joys, the worries, the love, and the chaos that children bring into life. I am indebted to my stepdad for that. Without him, it's possible that I would have never experienced motherhood.

I know this story is relevant to many, because infertility is a hot topic. Plus, now more than ever, an increasing number of women are having children later in life. I have shared this story with thousands of women, and, without fail, I always get feedback that it helped someone else go for their dream.

Common Beliefs to Disrupt:

- What's wrong with me that my life ended up like this?
- I'm stuck.
- I'm too old.
- I can't get it right.
- Nothing ever works for me.
- It's no use. I might as well accept it.

- There's nothing I can do about it.
- I don't deserve this.
- My body betrayed me.
- It's too hard.

Discover Your Why

Right now, there is something that gives your life a sense of meaning and purpose. It might be something you already have, or it could be something that you are striving for.

Perhaps it is finding a relationship. Maybe getting in the best shape of your life. It could be finding financial freedom. Getting a promotion at work or launching a business. Maybe it is having a family.

That thing you really want is your Why. It is the thing that you will always strive for, even on the hardest, most stressful days. Once you discover what your Why is, allow it to put you in your power place. Your power place is where great things happen, because you won't take no for an answer.

Everyone has a Why. If you don't know what yours is, I encourage you to ask yourself, "What is so important to me that I will never give up on making it happen?"

I have pondered that question a lot in my lifetime. While I had some idea of what I wanted, I wasn't always convinced I could have it. For one thing, I didn't always feel worthy. I didn't believe it could be me that would be so fortunate to have the life I really wanted. I was ready to settle for something less.

In other words, I was dreaming small, and I often felt stuck.

If you're always thinking you are stuck and convinced you can't find a way to get out of a situation, those thoughts will become your reality.

If you think luck will never come your way, it won't. If you believe you'll never be wealthy, you're right.

You'll never have any of those things if you say you won't. Why? Because if you don't believe it, you won't get into inspired action to even see if it is a possibility.

If you don't think you can run a marathon, you won't start to train for one.

If you don't think you can lose 20 pounds, you won't change your eating habits.

And if you don't think you can land your dream job or find your passion and purpose, you won't … because you won't even try.

If that sounds like you, it's time to thought swap. I'm not talking about doing a little about face. Oh no, I'm talking about a full-on high-in-the-sky double flip that will get things rolling.

Let's look at ways to thought swap, so that you get your heart pumping and motivated to go for your dreams.

Instead of saying, "I don't know how to do it," say, "I can learn how to do it."

Instead of saying, "I always procrastinate and never get anything done," say, "I am going to find something that matters to me more than anything, and then I am going to take it step by step."

Instead of saying, "I'm a failure," say, "I've learned a new lesson! When I become a huge success, that failure is going to make for one heck of a story."

Instead of saying, "My best days are behind me," say, "My best days are yet to come."

Instead of believing only others are born with special gifts, say, "God doesn't make mistakes. He created me and my uniqueness, and I am excited to find out where my talents take me."

Instead of saying I can't, say I can…

Lessons to Learn:

Going back to the common myths to dispel, let's take a look at the lessons that need to be learned so you can begin to pivot those disbeliefs that are holding you back.

- I trust God's divine plan for my life.
- If I give up, I'll never know what is possible.
- I feel better and better each day.
- I can do anything if it's important enough to me.
- I am only committed to Plan A for my life.
- I don't know what can happen if I try, but if I don't try, nothing will.
- For every problem, there are at least three solutions.
- I deserve every desire in my heart.
- My body knows exactly what to do.
- I am willing to be solution focused, versus problem focused.

Know that you are capable of anything. Know that you can study and commit to learning from those before you. And that you can become a great person in your own right.

Every day, look in the mirror and say:

- I am strong.
- I am a kind person.
- I am committed and determined.
- I am limitless.
- I can have anything I want.
- I can be whomever I want.
- I am a person of integrity.
- I am growing more each day.
- I am a good person.
- I deserve good things.
- I can have the wealth of my choice.

- I will have the wealth of my choice.
- I do deserve abundance.
- I can have the health of my choice.
- I will have the health of my choice.
- I am worthy.
- I am more than worthy.
- I can make a huge difference in other's lives.
- I am making that difference now.

You are the one and only person with the power to control your thoughts and put self-imposed limitations on your life. Your beliefs are your limits. How far will they take you?

Your beliefs are your limits. How far will they take you?

I guarantee that you determine your destiny–not your parents, not your siblings, not your employer. You alone control your destiny, and you are one thought away from being one step closer to it.

Are your thoughts telling you that you can … or are they telling you that you can't have your dream life?

Think about it. Transform it. Then let your thoughts guide your way.

One Thought Away

CAN'T IS NOT IN MY VOCABULARY

It is YOU who determines your destiny—not your parents, siblings, employer, or anyone else. You are one thought away from being one step closer to the life you want when you do this work. Are your thoughts telling you that you can or that you can't have your dream life?

Think about it. Then let your thoughts guide your way.

PART 1

1 Common Belief To Disrupt: What's wrong with me that my life ended up like this?
Lesson To Learn: I trust God's divine plan for my life.

2 Common Belief To Disrupt: I'm stuck.
Lesson To Learn: If I give up, I'll never know what is possible.

3 Common Belief To Disrupt: I'm too old.
Lesson To Learn: I feel better and better each day.

4 Common Belief To Disrupt: I can't get it right.
Lesson To Learn: I can do anything if it's important enough to me.

5 Common Belief To Disrupt: Nothing ever works for me.
Lesson To Learn: I am only committed to Plan A for my life.

#onethoughtaway | support@kerrytepedino.com | www.onethoughtawaybook.com

CHAPTER 9

One Thought Away

CAN'T IS NOT IN MY VOCABULARY

It is YOU who determines your destiny—not your parents, siblings, employer, or anyone else. You are one thought away from being one step closer to the life you want when you do this work. Are your thoughts telling you that you can or that you can't have your dream life?

Think about it. Then let your thoughts guide your way.

PART 2

6 Common Belief To Disrupt: It's no use. I might as well accept it.
Lesson To Learn: I don't know what can happen if I try, but if I don't try, nothing will.

7 Common Belief To Disrupt: There's nothing I can do about it.
Lesson To Learn: For every problem, there are at least three solutions.

8 Common Belief To Disrupt: I don't deserve this.
Lesson To Learn: I deserve every desire in my heart.

9 Common Belief To Disrupt: My body betrayed me.
Lesson To Learn: My body knows exactly what to do.

10 Common Belief To Disrupt: It's too hard.
Lesson To Learn: I am willing to be solution focused, versus problem focused.

#onethoughtaway | support@kerrytepedino.com | www.onethoughtawaybook.com

Chapter Ten

I'd Rather be Invisible

"That's why we sail. So, our children can grow up and be proud of whom they are. We are healing our souls by reconnecting to our ancestors. As we voyage, we are creating new stories within the tradition of the old stories; we are literally creating a new culture out of the old."

Those words were spoken by world-renowned navigator, Nainoa Thompson, and I believe that my grandmother influenced him to use his voice and leadership abilities to influence others.

My grandmother, Mabel Hefty, who was President Obama's teacher, was also the teacher for Nainoa Thompson, the famous navigator and President of the Polynesian Voyager Society.

Nainoa is the first Hawaiian to practice the ancient Polynesian art of navigation. It has been in use since the 14th century, from Hawaii to other Polynesian islands. It is navigation without the use of western instruments.

Nainoa may not have made his mark in history if it weren't for the influence my grandmother had in shaping him. She helped him to have confidence in himself and allow himself to be seen.

At the end of his fifth-grade school year, Nainoa won the Most Improved Award. He was to receive it at the final school ceremony. But there was one problem—Nainoa was shy and very self-conscious. He was reluctant to call attention to himself and he did not want to accept the award publicly.

Knowing that he would probably try to skip the ceremony, so he would not have to walk across the stage, my grandma called his mother and made sure Nainoa would be there.

Nainoa did attend the ceremony, reluctantly. He walked across that stage to accept his award, and in doing so, he found a different sense of pride in himself and discovered he was capable of doing more than he'd thought.

If Nainoa was still hiding, playing safe, and not stepping into his potential, I wonder if he would have rewritten Hawaiian navigation history. I wonder if he would be a role model for others, showing them what is possible.

Was that the pivotal moment that gave Nainoa the confidence to put himself in the spotlight, rather than sitting back, hoping that he wouldn't call attention to himself?

My grandmother was an observant teacher, and she could identify the potential issues that impacted her students. She stood for their potential and battled their insecurities. Whether it was a lack of self-esteem, shyness, insecurity, or a strong desire to be invisible, she helped them understand they were made for more.

Some of these are the very issues that come between the person we are and the person we have the potential to be.

Common Beliefs to Disrupt:

- It's not safe to be seen.
- What if people laugh at me?

- Perhaps my success was a fluke?
- I don't deserve this.
- Nobody else believes I deserve this.
- It would be so much better if nobody called attention to me.
- I just can't do this.

Many of the old, stale beliefs that we tell ourselves cause us to hold ourselves back from our greatness. If we don't have an incredible teacher, like my Tutu, that will call your mom to make sure you aren't playing hooky to not receive your award, then it is very easy to let our fears and insecurities hold us back.

Rewriting the history of your life is possible. You can overcome the beliefs that hold you back. You can step out of your comfort zone. You may even find that what's on the other side of your fear isn't scary at all. It might even be incredibly amazing!

We can dive in and disrupt the common beliefs that are holding you back. You can walk across the stage of your life, be acknowledged, and step into your potential.

I know that whatever you are fearing could happen, but it's often unlikely. If you succeed once, you can do it again. Allow yourself to bask in the glow of success. Feel it. Enjoy it. Let it strengthen you and inspire you to do it again!

Do a Thought Swap

If you're plagued by negative thoughts, it's time for a Thought Swap. Out with the old, and in with the new. It's your thoughts that have the most impact on your success, and until you change those thoughts, nothing different will happen. Yesterday's results will be today's and tomorrow's, as well.

So, what are Thought Swaps? Thought Swaps are taking one thought and turning it around. We want to focus on a thought that keeps you stuck and turn it into a thought that gets you excited and into a different energy of what is possible.

For example...

THOUGHT: What if I'm not successful?

THOUGHT SWAP: What if I am more successful than I ever thought possible?

THOUGHT: What if I'm rejected by others?

THOUGHT SWAP: What if finding my community is easier than I thought it could be?

You may know that Louise Hay didn't start Hay House until she was 60 years old. And she started it because she was diagnosed with cancer. She healed herself naturally from cancer and then wanted to get the message out to help others. This led her to be the founder and owner of one of the biggest publishing houses for personal development influencers. Louise Hay changed the world by staying on top of the way she thought, and it all happened at a dark and fearful time in her life.

If Louise Hay and Nainoa Thompson could change the trajectory of their lives (and the lives of so many around them), what can you do if you get curious and interested as to what's holding you back in your life?

Here's the thing—you can go for it ... or not.

If you go for it, you'll soon know how it can change your life. If you don't, you could spend the rest of your life wondering what could have happened if only you'd spoken up, stood on that stage, or let the world and yourself know just what you are capable of.

When you don't disrupt the thoughts and beliefs that are holding you back, there could come a day where you will regret it. That little voice in your head will question what could have, would have, and should have been. And the voice of regret will nag you, reminding you of what may have happened, if only …

That monkey mind is super sneaky! But to us, especially when we have convinced ourselves that we aren't worthy, it can sound really logical. It sounds logical because it's an easier route. It's way more comfortable to stay in the status quo, where we know you're safe and protected, than it is to put yourself out there and subject ourselves to all of the possibilities that our mind has conjured up.

What happens, though, when you change your thoughts and take that first step toward who you really want to be?

It's like learning to ride a bike. You start off on training wheels, and you feel safe. But then, one day, it's time to ride your bike without that safety net. The training wheels are off, but you find that you're too scared to give it a go.

So, your mom or dad held onto the bike, to give you reassurance that they wouldn't let you fall. Then comes the time when they let go, and you ride solo. You can refuse to try, or you can give it a try and see what happens.

Sure, it's shaky at first, scary even. And if you fall, it might hurt a little. But yet you get back on, finding that with the second time, it's just a little easier. Then the third, fourth, and fifth attempt … and you're off.

The really cool thing is that as you master riding that bike without training wheels, you find you're not scared anymore. Heck, you're even good at it! And the more you do it, the less you even think about falling. It's as if riding a bike is as easy as walking.

With each bike ride, you gain confidence. Then, one day, you surprise yourself by saying, "Look, Mom! No hands!"

That's what happens when you put yourself out there in the bigger picture of your life and take the first step to do what you didn't think you could do.

Each time you dispel those limiting beliefs that reside in your mind, you put yourself in a position to make new decisions. You take a different course of action than you would have taken before. When that happens, you reprioritize your thoughts. They support the things you want to do and the person you want to be.

You find that you're in a different season—a different stage of your growth and your life.

> Your thoughts support the things you want to do and the person you want to be.

I'm the CEO of a significant business. I'm a mother, daughter, sister, mentor and a friend to many. I have a very healthy relationship with God. I make the time for the things that are important to me, and you can, too.

It's up to you. You're one thought away from letting fear control your life. You're also one thought away from getting on that bike and giving it your best shot.

Allow yourself the flexibility to renegotiate and pivot along the way. Take the pressure off of yourself from needing to know all the answers or needing to get it right the first time. And know that nothing is set in stone. There is absolutely no guarantee that you'll fail.

There is no guarantee that someone will laugh at you or think you're being ridiculous. Remember the last chapter? "Can't" is not a sure thing. Don't kid yourself into believing that it is.

Yes, it will take some thought reinforcement in order to step out of your comfort zone. Give yourself the support you need. Allow yourself the space and the wiggle room to breathe. Relax into your humanness as you pioneer new territory for yourself.

And have fun doing it! Too often, we take the stretch outside of our comfort zone so seriously. This doesn't have to be intense. It can be adventurous and playful. You can even give yourself permission to enjoy it.

Laugh at yourself if you want to. Just don't convince yourself that it's not worth the effort to stretch. Because it most definitely is.

It's your life that is placed on hold when you don't allow yourself to work on your thinking, impacting your goals and dreams. While you might have to consider other people, like your partner, spouse, or kids, it is ultimately you that will pay the price if you put your wants on a shelf. Don't get off course. Because nothing gets better until you take action.

You would never ask someone you love to ditch their dreams, would you? Of course not. So why would you talk yourself out of your own dreams by putting others first … and yourself last?

Remember, the happier you are and the closer you get to reaching your potential, the better you will be for everyone—yourself, your spouse, kids, parents, coworkers, employees, everyone.

Be patient and compassionate with yourself. The beliefs that will be demanded for you to dispel didn't pop up in your head overnight. They've been there for a long time, and it's going to take a consistent, conscious, and committed effort to heal them. It'll require that you learn some valuable lessons.

Lessons to Learn:
- I am safe. Breathe.
- I am proud of who I am, and that's what matters most.
- If I did it once, I can do it again.
- I worked hard for this; it's okay to be recognized.
- I respect the opinion of others, but it doesn't have to influence my own opinion.
- I have something of value to contribute to others. I get to

overcome my fears in order to do so.

- I can do anything I set my mind to.

You're retraining yourself to think differently—this time, in a way that will support and benefit your goals.

One good way to do that is to visualize what your life will look like tomorrow, next week, next month or a year from now. How about five years from now?

Visualize it in your mind's eye every morning and every night. Picture where you'll be, what you'll be doing, feel into it. Experience the peace within yourself, your newfound pride, and the inner confidence that comes from conquering your monkey mind. Own what you're capable of.

You will prevail.
You will overcome.
You will win.

Whatever you're thinking and visualizing is going to become your reality. You are only one thought away.

The most successful athletes in the world visualize their win even before they tie their shoes and step onto the court. They experience the exhilaration, joy, and pride of winning before they even begin. Then their mind—their thoughts—go to work to make that happen.

Visualization gets you comfortable with the unknown. It helps to make the invisible visible, at least in your mind's eye.

As they say, when you can see it, you can believe it.

You can believe that you can find the nerve to step across the stage and let the world watch as you accept the award for doing what you never thought possible.

You can believe that you can keep that bike upright when your parents let go.

You can believe that this time you will not fall.

You will prevail.

You will overcome.

You will win.

To get there, you get to start somewhere. Start with your thoughts. They're the one thing that has kept you in limbo, held you back, and kept you from stepping into your greatness.

Your thoughts might be invisible to the world around you, but your potential doesn't have to be.

One Thought Away

I'D RATHER BE INVISIBLE

Many of the old, stale beliefs that we tell ourselves cause us to hold ourselves back from our greatness. Rewriting the history of your life is possible. You can overcome the beliefs that hold you back. You can step out of your comfort zone. You may even find that what's on the other side of your fear isn't scary at all. It might even be incredibly amazing!

Whatever you're thinking and visualizing is going to become your reality. Let's be strategic in our thinking.

PART 1

1 Common Belief To Disrupt: It's not safe to be seen.
Lesson To Learn: I am safe. Breathe.

2 Common Belief To Disrupt: What if people laugh at me?
Lesson To Learn: I am proud of who I am and that's what matters most.

3 Common Belief To Disrupt: Perhaps my success was a fluke?
Lesson To Learn: If I did it once, I can do it again.

4 Common Belief To Disrupt: I don't deserve this.
Lesson To Learn: I worked hard for this, it's okay to be recognized.

#onethoughtaway | support@kerrytepedino.com | www.onethoughtawaybook.com

CHAPTER 10

One Thought Away

I'D RATHER BE INVISIBLE

Many of the old, stale beliefs that we tell ourselves cause us to hold ourselves back from our greatness. Rewriting the history of your life is possible. You can overcome the beliefs that hold you back. You can step out of your comfort zone. You may even find that what's on the other side of your fear isn't scary at all. It might even be incredibly amazing!

Whatever you're thinking and visualizing is going to become your reality. Let's be strategic in our thinking.

PART 2

5 Common Belief To Disrupt: Nobody else believes I deserve this.
Lesson To Learn: I respect the opinion of others, but it doesn't have to influence my own opinion.

6 Common Belief To Disrupt: It would be so much better if nobody called attention to me.
Lesson To Learn: I have something of value to contribute. I get to overcome my fears in order to do so.

7 Common Belief To Disrupt: I just can't do this.
Lesson To Learn: I can do anything I set my mind to.

#onethoughtaway | support@kerrytepedino.com | www.onethoughtawaybook.com

Chapter Eleven

Jump and the Net Will Appear

"I can't do this. There is absolutely no way," I told myself as I came face to face with one of my biggest fears.

And that fear stayed with me for years.

Between my junior and senior year in college, I moved to Maui with a group of friends for the summer. When I wasn't working on a whale watching boat, I hung out with a bunch of friends, some of which were always ready to do the next impromptu crazy thing.

One day, I was off work when a couple of friends decided that we all needed to go jump Black Rock, a cliff made out of jagged lava rocks that plunged into the ocean. Sounds intriguing, right? To me, it sounded horrifying.

But I didn't dare tell anyone how scared I was. Out of fear of being judged, I went along with the idea, even attempting to act excited, although the mere thought of jumping Black Rock left me sick to my stomach.

Arriving at the beach, warm sand between my toes, I watched as my friends threw caution to the wind and ran to the edge of the cliff.

Me? I froze.

"I can't do this. I don't have what it takes," my inner voice said.

In that moment, I convinced myself that I wasn't brave or courageous. I wasn't as fun or as cool as my friends. I was lacking.

While I really wanted to fit in and be accepted by my friends, I was paralyzed, totally unable to take that giant leap of faith and jump off the rock. Even if I wanted to, I knew there was no way I could bring myself to do it.

As I watched my friends climb the cliff and jump into the beautiful blue water, I created a belief in my head, "I don't have what it takes to do hard things."

So, I didn't. I didn't jump off Black Rock. That thought and decision impacted me for many years to come.

Fast forward 20 years, I was back in Maui to attend a business conference. When we walked into our hotel room, I went straight out the balcony to see our view. Boom! Black Rock was staring me straight in the face!

Oh, the irony.

The next day I was outside visiting with friends from the conference, and one of them mentioned a videographer would be taping him doing some cliff jumps. I told him that I used to live in Maui and had almost jumped Black Rock, but I'd chickened out.

"You should jump it with me," JR said.

I laughed that off. "Thank you, but no thank you."

He got serious and his tone changed. He repeated it, this time more serious.

"Kerry, you *should* jump it with me."

It didn't sound like a suggestion.

I knew in that moment that I was getting a second chance to rewrite my story and reprogram my mind. It was an opportunity to recreate myself as someone who was brave and courageous.

I knew that I couldn't teach about facing one's fears with full integrity if I didn't take that leap. It was critical for me to change my beliefs about what I could do and what was possible.

I changed into my bathing suit and grabbed my towel. JR and I made the short walk to the beach, with my knees knocking the entire time. Barefoot, I climbed up the sharp lava rock, and it felt treacherous.

When I got to the jumping point, I was holding on to JR's hand for dear life as I inched my toes to the cliff's edge.

Then, I took a deep, deep breath and reminded myself that this was my second chance.

One, two, three! I jumped! All the way down yelling, "BELIEVE!!!!"

The water was so warm and beautiful. I was surrounded by fish and vibrant coral. It was so captivating. It was so much more beautiful than I imagined. And it was not that scary!

I'd deprived myself of this experience and believing in myself on this level for 20 years. I couldn't believe it.

JR jumped and we swam back to shore. We hustled back over to our friends, and I shared, "I did it!!!" With a lot of high fives and hugs, I was feeling pure inspiration move through my veins and blurted out, "You guys should do it, too!"

I got crickets.

No one said a word.

I knew exactly what they were feeling, and I was determined to stand for their breakthrough, the way JR had stood for mine. I got a commitment from a group of 12 friends and the next morning we met bright and early at 7am at the beach.

As we climbed up the cliffs, this time everyone wearing shoes, we helped each other to the top, as a community. Since I was the instigator, I jumped first, showing everybody that they were going to be okay.

It was me this time who let others know that they could do hard things. That they could push through their fears and overcome them, just like I had.

As I treaded water in the beautiful blue water and watched each friend take their leap of faith, I cheered them on and felt so proud of them.

There's nothing like community to help us get through those harder moments. It takes connection with others who believe in us, even when we don't quite believe in ourselves yet, for us to push to our next level.

Whenever I crack a code and push myself to my next level, I feel a sense of responsibility to help others do the same. To push any limiting thinking around "I can't" and expand their beliefs in themselves, just like JR stood for me.

I know that millions of people hold themselves back due to fear. With the proper support, they could jump and realize there is a net there to catch them, too. It's been there all along; they just need a little help to see it.

Common Beliefs to Disrupt:

- I failed in the past.
- It's too scary.
- I don't have what it takes.
- I'm not ready.
- That's way too far out of my comfort zone.

Taking a Second Chance

My lack of courage on that day impacted the way I thought about myself for many years. At the time, I didn't have the same level of skill set to stretch outside of my comfort zone and do hard, scary things.

Guess what? Whatever your stretch is, that's your cliff. That's your black rock that you've been paralyzed and unable to jump off and away from … until now.

When I finally did jump off Black Rock, at the age of 47, I was still scared. I still felt sick to my stomach, and I didn't want to jump, but I knew I had to take Black Rock on if I wanted to teach others to stretch, too.

I reluctantly chose to be an example of what is possible, first for myself, second for my family, and third for my friends, clients, peers, and anyone I would have the honor to impact.

I got a second chance to make that fearful jump off Black Rock. I now look at second chances as invitations to change my negative preconceptions into powerfully positive outcomes.

In doing so, I discovered that the jump wasn't the hardest part—it was the fear that enveloped my body before the jump. It was the space of the unexpected. In comparison, the jump was easy. It was like freeing myself from the self-induced chains that had been holding me back for 20 long years.

What chains have been holding you back and kept you from the life you want? When you face and release the fears of the unknown, you've found something invaluable. You've found freedom.

This is your second chance.

It's your second chance at every single dream that you have ever said was important to you, but you were scared to make it happen.

When you finally face that fear and take the leap, it's life changing.

When I took that jump off Black Rock, I was overjoyed. I did it! And not only did I do it, but I knew without a doubt that I'd do it again.

It was such a rush, a feeling of accomplishment, that I immediately wanted to stand for others to jump, too. I wanted them to jump past their own fears, because I had the confirmation again that there's a lot of life beyond our fears, and it was totally worth jumping for.

There's a whole world available to you beyond the jump. It's the climb to the top of the cliff and teetering at the edge with your toes hanging over the side that's the hardest part.

It's that moment of hesitation that can completely define who you believe yourself to be. It's not until you allow yourself to jump that you give yourself a chance to stretch beyond your limitations. When you do, you become limitless.

> There's a lot of life beyond your fears.

With each lesson learned, you break yet another limit or fear that is holding you back. And you get to become courageous enough to do courageous things.

Lessons to Learn:

- This is my second chance.
- If not now, then when?
- There is no time like the present.
- Jump and the net will appear.

There's a whole world of courageous acts for you to choose to do. It doesn't matter what they are—what is courageous to one person might not feel like a big deal to another, and vice versa. Forget about everyone else and what they think. Focus on what stretches you and pushes you beyond your limitations.

Remember, too, that it is right before you experience your big breakthrough that you have the most difficulty. That's when your monkey mind will try to talk you out of going to the next level, telling you not to take that leap. Don't let that get in your way. The storm usually gets thicker before the rainbow breaks.

What's Your Black Rock?

Are you terrified to be vulnerable with another person? Scared to launch a new business or go for that promotion you secretly want? Or it could be something as simple, and vital, as putting yourself before your children for once.

Whatever your fear, your jump is the piece that you get to face and conquer in order to stretch and expand. Remember those neurons and new connections in your brain we talked about earlier? That's what's at play here. You're rewriting them, and in the process, you're rewriting a different life story with an upgraded ending.

Think of it as the art of telling a different story of your life. When you tell the new story to yourself, you're training your brain to think it into reality. The more you tell the new story, it becomes a part of your cellular makeup, your world starts to shift, and opens up for you in ways that you never imagined.

Your life can be even bigger than you are imagining now, and here's why: You don't yet know how to think *that* big. And you won't until you jump and go all in.

When I started this journey, I didn't have the capacity to dream as big as my life has currently gotten. But now I know that I can dream even bigger. I know what I'm capable of, and it's no longer scary. It's actually quite thrilling to imagine what I can do each time I step out of my comfort zone again.

If I can do it, you can do it, too.

Being Your Own Positive Reinforcement

As you continue on this path and build yourself, you'll get positive reinforcement—from yourself.

"Wow, I accomplished that goal. It was hard, but I did it! I achieved that dream. And it wasn't as hard as I thought it would be."

"I'm so proud that I took that on. I didn't even know I could create such amazing results."

The list could go on and on.

As you're consistent with this, the connectors and neurons in your brain are getting stronger to the new bigger, expansive story of your life. In turn, your dreams get bigger and more expansive.

See how that works? Pretty cool, huh?

You start to realize that you can find true love after a heartbreak or that there is life after losing someone you adored.

You realize that you can rebuild financial freedom after a bankruptcy.

That healing is possible after a scary diagnosis.

Whatever it is that you didn't think possible, can happen for you. For it to happen, though, you get to be in the game playing full out. Stretch your limits. Jump your Black Rock.

Whatever your Black Rock is, you can conquer it. Sometimes the dream we want the most is right in front of us, but we push it away because of fear.

This is a great time to get curious and interested. Because your fears will follow you wherever you go, whether it's a different cliff, a new relationship, or another career. Those things are just geography. Fears don't reside anywhere—they follow us.

We might fear that others will judge us, but did it ever occur to you that the fear stems from the fact that we are judging ourselves? Our overactive imagination then convinces us that, of course, others will judge us, too. But all too often, that's an invalid assumption. It's a fear that doesn't actually happen. Yet, we let it hold us back.

At the same time, it reinforces those common beliefs—the ones we really want to dispel. Those beliefs have us convinced that we aren't risk takers, that we're too old, too timid, too frightened to take a leap of faith.

Second chances give us an opportunity to reprogram our stinking thinking and rewrite our endings.

What if your new thinking, your swapped thoughts, sounded more like…

- I can do anything—watch me!
- Sure, I might be afraid, but I'm going to do it, anyway.
- I'm only too old if I'm dead.
- I have no expectations because I don't know what to expect. So, in times of uncertainty, anything is possible.
- What do I have to lose?
- I trust myself.
- I get to live the life I've always secretly wanted.
- I choose to take the courageous path.
- Why put off living my dream life?
- Tomorrow is not guaranteed.

What's your second chance? What are you willing to do to make it happen?

More important, what is it costing you until you do?

All it takes is one thought … you are one thought away from taking that jump and proving to yourself that you can transform your life.

It's a thought that can change everything … if you're willing to take it.

CHAPTER 11

One Thought Away

JUMP AND THE NET WILL APPEAR

What chains have been holding you back and kept you from the life you want? When you face and release the fears of the unknown, you've found something invaluable. You've found freedom.

All it takes is one thought. You are one thought away from taking that jump and proving to yourself that you can transform your life.

It's a thought that can change everything ... if you're willing to take it.

1 Common Belief To Disrupt: I failed in the past.
Lesson To Learn: This is my second chance.

2 Common Belief To Disrupt: It's too scary.
Lesson To Learn: If not now, then when?

3 Common Belief To Disrupt: I don't have what it takes.
Lesson To Learn: I trust myself.

4 Common Belief To Disrupt: I'm not ready.
Lesson To Learn: There is no time like the present.

5 Common Belief To Disrupt: That's way too far out of my comfort zone.
Lesson To Learn: Jump and the net will appear.

#onethoughtaway | support@kerrytepedino.com | www.onethoughtawaybook.com

Chapter Twelve

The Split-Second Moment of Hesitation

W e all have the power of choice in everything we do. That choice requires first a thought. That thought can also produce something else—a moment of hesitation. It's a split-second moment where you face the choices you have, and you either do what you have always done, or you do something different.

While some choices may be pondered for days, weeks, or even months, the hesitation I'm referring to is the one immediately prior to making our decision. I refer to it as the "split-second moment of hesitation" because it happens so fast.

It's that passing moment when you're standing at a fork in the road, and you know if you choose the path you've always taken, nothing will change. Or you can make a different choice, one that will take you on a path you've never traveled, but one that will give you a different result.

The new and different choices feel risky. They can also be exciting. Likely, they will produce a mixture of different feelings and emotions.

Some decisions and choices we make might be fast. Others take time, such as getting married, changing careers, or moving thousands of miles from everything and everyone we know.

Moments of Hesitation

Still, there are those decisions that might appear small at the time but end up changing the trajectory of our lives. I've provided examples of many in the previous chapters. Whether it's walking across a stage or getting up off the bathroom floor and committing to stop the self-sabotage. The mere choice to change often comes with a moment of hesitation.

You are one thought away from staying stuck, just as you are one thought away from changing your entire life.

Changing the way I thought gave me permission to believe in myself and the mission I am fulfilling today. I've put myself out on a limb and exposed my fears and challenges. I took a risk to change my life, and I'm now committed to using the lessons I learned to help you.

What I have observed is that moments of hesitation are often fueled by fear, so we hesitate. In that moment, it will be demanded of us to get past that internal fear. It will take a moment of great strength to do something different than we have always done before.

The possibility of failure might seem like a huge deterrent to making a change. But what's really interesting is that I've discovered failure isn't the only thing on that list. Success is.

People are afraid of success. What if they get what they want, only to later lose it? What if they are successful, then realize that it didn't make them happy at all?

There are a lot of what ifs that can rear their ugly heads in that moment of hesitation. They can be so consuming that they paralyze us from making a choice at all, whether it is good for us or not.

Renowned psychologist Dr. Smiley Blanton once said that fear is the most subtle and destructive of all human diseases. I agree.

Fear kills dreams. Fear kills hope. It puts people in the hospital. It can age you. Fear can hold you back from doing something that you know you are capable of doing. It will paralyze you and put you under its hypnotic spell.

Many of us cling to our fears. We've invested our time and energy into our fears for so long that we have trained ourselves to think there must be a benefit to having them. Otherwise, we wouldn't listen to our fears and give them power.

> Change requires growth. Growth requires change.

The only benefit is that fear keeps us from the unknown, a place of uncertainty. In our mind, the unknown is a place to avoid.

One of the reasons many of us don't take the next step or make a different choice is because we simply don't know how to. Or because subconsciously we don't believe we deserve more.

But to get beyond the lacking result, we must be brave enough to let go of these ways of resistance. The truth is we are one thought away from our dreams becoming a reality. Of course, that doesn't happen with a wink and a nod. It requires our participation and effort. For many, it's a process that is foreign territory. We don't invest in ourselves and our dreams, and we don't know how.

To find out if you're ready to break through the hesitation that holds you back, ask yourself the following questions:

- How much time do you spend working on you?
- How much time do you spend every day working on your dream?
- How much time have you spent doing that in the last 90 days?
- What kind of investment have you made in you?

As you begin to look at where you want to go, you get to make a conscious effort to work on your own development. Change requires growth. The opposite is also true. Growth requires change.

If fear is holding you back, learn what you can do to overcome it. Find the key that will motivate you to take your jump off of your Black Rock.

If you're stuck in the status quo because you have limited vision, it's time to get the support and skills to paint the picture of your dream. It's said you can't hit a target that you can't see. The same is true for dreams.

It's time to pivot and stop asking what could go wrong if you do make a different choice. Instead, start asking what would happen if you don't make a different choice.

Let me explain.

Motivational speaker Les Brown was driving home from his friend's funeral, and he was thinking about all the things his friend had wanted to do, but never got to do. His friend wasn't old and didn't get a chance to live a ripe old age. As Les realized the things his friend didn't have the chance to experience or accomplish, his reflection put him in a place of curiosity about his own life.

What hadn't he done yet that he wanted to do before he died? How had he held himself back? What excuses had he made for not taking a leap or getting started? What conditions had he placed on his dreams?

And what was stopping him from checking off his bucket list of dreams starting immediately?

Put yourself in Les's shoes. What are the things you wish you had done in your life? What are the things that you want to do while you still have the chance?

Stop hesitating. The best thing to do is to get started. Stop making excuses. Don't put conditions on your dreams. If you know that not going for your dream is something you'll regret when your time on earth is done, it's time to choose a different path and make it happen.

Take action, no matter how small. Any action forward is in the direction of that dream, that goal, or that vision is productive action. Even if it's a baby step that you do today, or a baby step that you take tomorrow, it's productive action, and it's moving you forward.

Give yourself permission to jump.

Oh, I know that it might not seem like the "right" time. There might even be obstacles and challenges that are like signs telling you to give up. You might try to convince yourself that it's not gonna happen, and the universe is trying to tell you to let that dream go.

I say that's just a sign to try harder. You are just getting tested on how important that goal, that dream, that vision really is for you.

I know. My biggest dream was tested, again and again, which was to have more kids. I even got pregnant and miscarried on the day before Christmas Eve, 2018.

I didn't give up.

I went back and started IVF rounds to make my dream a reality.

Then COVID hit, and all the IVF clinics were shut down. My dream was on lockdown.

It sure could have been easy to give up on my dream. A lot of people would have. But thankfully, I had the tools to keep me focused, on track, and hooked on the vision of what I wanted.

I never lost sight of my dream, and no matter how much adversity I encountered, I wasn't going to let it get me to the breaking point. On the contrary, the adversity I faced only made my desire stronger.

In those moments as you summon your strength, you're going to need to dive deep into your heart and remind yourself that you are a powerful, brave, courageous person in this world. Whatever your dream is, know that it's worth going for. It's worth fighting for. It's the good fight.

Yes, you are worthy of it. You are deserving enough to have your dream.

The split-second moment of hesitation that you take before deciding to pursue your dream is a defining moment in your transformational journey.

Use that moment to see your vision. Let yourself dream like you've never dreamed before. Dream without inhibitions. Then choose the path least traveled—the path where dreams come true.

You are just a split second thought away from having what you really want.

One Thought Away

THE SPLIT-SECOND MOMENT OF HESITATION

We all have the power of choice in everything we do. That choice requires first a thought. That thought can also produce something else—a moment of hesitation. It's a split-second moment where you face the choices you have, and you either do what you have always done, or you do something different.

You are just a split second moment away from a better life.

1) Why are you still making choices that don't serve you?

2) What beliefs do you get to disrupt to get a positive, different result?

3) What are the lessons to learn by changing those beliefs/thoughts?

#onethoughtaway | support@kerrytepedino.com | www.onethoughtawaybook.com

Chapter Thirteen

Common Ways of Self-Sabotage

We've talked about making changes in your life...

Perhaps you want to switch careers or open a business. Maybe you need to find the confidence to walk away from an abusive relationship. You might want to turn your financial wellbeing around for you and your family. Perhaps you want to lose weight and improve your health.

Whatever your goal or dream is, it is one thought away. It all starts with a thought that plants the seed in your mind to make the changes and take the action to make it happen.

I commend you for having that thought, expressing it, and believing in it. Because without that one single thought, nothing will happen. With it, you've given yourself permission to turn that one thought into big, life-changing results.

Switching our mindset and beliefs puts the gear in motion and propels us to take action toward our dreams. Initially, that's motivating. We want to make a change, and we're energized and pumped up about doing it. But as we've seen throughout our lives, the excitement and confidence that we feel at the onset of making those changes wanes as time goes on.

We make excuses for not taking action today, promising ourselves that tomorrow is another day.

What could happen is you don't see the results you want when you want them, and discouragement sets in. When that happens, your thoughts shift from "1 can do this" to "This is too hard" or "It'll never happen, so why even try?"

Or we convince ourselves that we can live with the status quo, for a little while, anyway. In other words, we procrastinate and put our dreams on hold.

You might even think things, such as...

- This is my lot in life. I might as well accept it and move on.
- They will never change, and I just have to live with that.
- I have too many other things to do.
- There's just no time for me—maybe when the kids grow up things will change.
- I'll never have enough money.

There are hundreds of excuses that we give for not taking action to grow that seed we planted. Every one of them is a form of self-sabotage.

The only one who can achieve your goals or make your dreams come true is *you*. You are the only one who can bring your dream to fruition. You are the only one who can suffocate it, and you are the only one who can resuscitate it.

It's human nature to start strong, being gung-ho about making exciting changes. It's also human nature when we encounter challenges or setbacks to return to our old ways of thinking. After all, that's what we know.

We also know that with change comes uncertainty—one of the biggest unknowns is what will happen if we succeed? And what will happen if we fail?

So, we start off like gangbusters, and then we lose steam. As soon as we lose steam, our thoughts become weaker. They take a lower priority in our day-to-day lives, and we fall back into our old ways of thinking and doing.

When that happens, our dream falls to the wayside, once again becoming nothing more than a wish … one without a genie in a bottle to grant it.

You are the only one who can grant your wish. Be your own genie, and stop self-sabotaging your dreams and goals. To do that, you have to keep your thought—you know the one, the thought that spurred you to want to create something new, something different, something exciting and positive in your life— keep that thought at the forefront of your mind.

This is your life. Don't self-sabotage it. Create it.

Don't let it slip from your grasp and fall asleep. Instead, grasp it, keep it wide awake, and breathe new life into it.

I get it. Like when running a marathon, we can often be strong starters, but weak finishers. We run out of gas. But there is a way to overcome that, and it is in the way you are thinking.

Every time you are strong and you reinforce the thought that spawned your dream, something magical happens. You give it life. It shows you that you do have what it takes to start strong and finish strong.

And every time you get another experience of yourself being that person who follows through, you recalibrate. You start to imagine yourself in a different way, as a strong finisher, not just now, but all the way to the finish line.

So, not only are you shifting the thoughts of what you want to create and do, but you're also shifting how you think about yourself.

Remember when I told you about my first attempt to jump off Black Rock and how petrified I was? I could have thrown caution to the wind and taken a leap, despite my fear, but my unserving beliefs snuck in, and I used them as excuses...

"No way! This is too scary. What if I die? What if they all laugh at me? I don't have it in me."

I'm sure you can imagine all of the ways my monkey mind worked to self-sabotage my first attempt to take a leap into the unknown.

Then, came my second attempt. I'd already been practicing One Thought Away, and I knew how powerful it could be. I knew that I had been allowing myself to be vulnerable, and I planted the thought of confidence in my mind that if my friend could jump, so could I.

That thought started out strong. Sure, I knew my fears were still there, but this time, I also knew that I had to debunk the personal myth in my mind that created self-imposed limitations. I could conquer my fears and claim victory over them. To do that, I had to keep my thoughts stronger than my doubts and fears.

And I did it! I was surprised to find how exhilarating and exciting it was! To think, though, that I could have just as easily talked myself out of it, just as I had the first time, made me think about where else I'd self-sabotaged myself in my life ... and what I could do to change that.

I discovered that I was one thought away from facing and overcoming any challenge before me. When I jumped off Black Rock, I changed my story. I showed myself that it is possible to be a strong starter and a strong finisher.

You can change your story, too. And you don't have to wait until the split second before you dive into the unknown to do it. You can start right now, at this very minute.

Self-sabotage is a habit. We pull excuses out of a hat whenever we're afraid of what could happen. It's a protective mechanism to keep us safe. It frees us from being responsible for our actions and outcomes. And it keeps us in our comfort zone, where we don't face the unknown that we too often perceive negatively.

That said, how do we change our story? How do we start strong and manage to stay strong, despite our tendency to self-sabotage our dreams? We feed ourselves positive thoughts that will provide us with the confidence and strength to see our desires through.

One thing you can do is to start and finish your day, every day, with the visualization of your dream or goal being achieved. In your mind's eye, know exactly how it feels and what it looks like the minute it happens. How will it change your life forever?

See every single detail with as much clarity as your mind can muster. Then, do it again that night … and then the next morning and the next night. Reinforcing your visualization makes it stronger. Plus, it puts your subconscious, which is where your thoughts are stored, to work to make them come true.

Here are a few examples of thoughts that can support you…

- I have the courage to face my fear.
- I have strong and loving relationships.
- I attract amazing people.
- I make a positive difference in the world around me.
- I see opportunity in every change.
- My body is fit and healthy.
- I am worthy.
- I am free of guilt and shame.

- I am a survivor!
- I am determined.
- I am stronger now than I have ever been.
- I've got this!

You get the idea—whatever it is you want comes with common beliefs to disrupt. Rather than committing self-sabotage, you can keep your dream alive by affirming it to already be so. With repetition, you buy into it, and your subconscious goes to work to make it happen for you, even as you sleep.

In essence, your thoughts are your strengths, and your strengths are your anchor. They're always there to keep you connected to what you want—that dominant thought that can, and will, change your outcomes.

Keep the positive thought alive. Feed it well, so it remains strong. Make it even stronger by affirming it and visualizing it as it becomes your reality. Let yourself experience how it feels to be real. Allow yourself to feel lighthearted, loved, secure, confident, thin, strong, courageous, exuberant … whatever your fulfilled dream makes you feel.

And let that counter self-sabotage the next time it creeps in, because it will.

Dreams don't come true overnight. They take time to achieve. It's going to take more than one day to make it happen. That's why I stress the importance of repetition and consistency. You get to reinforce and strengthen your thoughts daily. You get to repeat your positive thoughts every day, every night, every week, and every month, so they become who you naturally are.

Creating a dream life takes time and planning. It requires positive thoughts backed by inspired action. Keep doing the work. Don't lose steam. Never let a self-defeating thought take you so off course that you lose sight of what you really want in life.

Your thoughts are impacting you 100% of the time. You get to be in the driver's seat and decide where they take you. You do have what it takes to shift anything in your life that feels like it's not on track. You now have the tools to course correct and stay on track for your dream life.

Allow yourself to go deeper into knowing what is possible for you. Commit to starting now. Start with positive thoughts, then visualize what you're creating in your life. See it. Feel it. Know how it feels to believe in yourself, love yourself, accept yourself, and support yourself.

Step into your next level of potential because everything is possible. You do have what it takes to breathe life into your dreams. You do have what it takes to master your mindset and your emotions. You have what it takes to learn from the past, let go of it, and get excited about your future.

This is your life.

Don't self-sabotage it—create it.

CHAPTER 13

One Thought Away

COMMON WAYS OF SELF-SABOTAGE

Your thoughts are impacting you 100% of the time. You get to be in the driver's seat and decide where they take you. You do have what it takes to shift anything in your life that does not feel on track. You now have the tools to course correct and stay on track for your dream life.

This is your life.
This is your future.
Don't self-sabotage it—create it.

What is the future I desire for my life that I am committed to creating?

Chapter Fourteen

Self-Care is Not a Luxury!

ut your oxygen mask on first, so you will be able to take care of others. We've all heard that saying, but we also know that as parents, spouses, caregivers, employees and employers, it's not uncommon to put ourselves last.

Sometimes, we even believe that it's selfish to take time for ourselves. We let ourselves think that setting aside a few minutes, hours, or even a day just for ourselves is inconsiderate of the needs of other people in our lives. After all, they need us, and it is our responsibility to take care of them and their needs.

I choose to look at this from another perspective. Self-love is not selfish at all. The way I view it, it's actually selfish if we don't take care of ourselves *first*. We need to take care of ourselves *before* we take care of others.

Here's why: if you aren't taking care of yourself, it is impossible to operate at full capacity. At best, you're probably operating at 50 percent. That means that when you're with your partner, spouse, kids, etc., you're only able to give them 50 percent—of yourself, your time, your attention, your interest, or your effort.

They're not getting all of you because you simply don't have it to give.

When you put yourself first, though, you're rested and rejuvenated. You're nurtured and healthy. You're relaxed.

Suffice it to say, self-love prevents overwhelm. When you give yourself that self-love, time, and attention, you're able to operate at your highest potential. You can be the happiest, healthiest version of you possible.

That's when you're able to operate at 100% most of the time.

Self-love is not selfish at all. It's one of the least selfish things you can do for yourself and your loved ones. To be able to give them the best you that you can give, to be able to give them 90 percent of your time, attention, and care by taking care of yourself is an incredible gift for all of you.

We've been conditioned to think differently, though. There are many who grew up with the responsibility of taking care of younger siblings. They've been charged with the responsibility of raising someone else. It was what it was, and now putting others first is a given.

Then, there are those who are now entrusted with caring for their aging parents, and they do so without giving it a second thought. Their loved ones are their priorities. They put themselves last, telling themselves that someday they'll take the time to go to the spa, take up golfing or hiking, enjoy a hobby, indulge in a nap, or spend time being anything other than a spouse, child, parent, or employer/employee.

There's a little problem with that thinking, though. Someday rarely comes. As soon as one responsibility is taken off our plate, something else is loaded onto it. And that is because we allow it to happen. Being needed has become a lifestyle.

If someday does come and a rare opportunity to do something "selfish" arises, by putting ourselves last, we aren't in a position to benefit from it. We're fatigued. We have high blood pressure, and our blood sugar is shot. Just as bad, we become so disconnected from our dreams that we don't even know what we want anymore.

There are so many consequences that stem from not allotting time to yourself *first*, and every one of them has a negative impact on you and on the people you love.

Think about it. You'd never tell your child or a loved one to let their dreams die. I know I wouldn't. But as a parent and a role model, that's exactly what you're doing when you let your own dreams die, putting them last and making everyone else's needs and wishes more important than your own.

Sacrificing your needs is a disservice to the people you love and to the people who love you. Don't you think they want you to be happy and healthy? Don't you think you're able to be a better role model, parent, or spouse when you know you have your oxygen mask on, so you have the capability of giving them the best you have to give?

> Self-love isn't selfish at all. It's selfless.

Do any of these scenarios ring a bell?

Profits are down at work, and you're under pressure to do whatever it takes to turn it around. You go in early and come home late, grabbing a bite to eat on the go. You haven't gone on your daily run in a couple weeks. And when you get home, you're so exhausted and stressed that you don't have the time or energy to play with your kids. It'll have to wait until things settle down.

Your best friend calls and asks you to go watch a movie with her — or get a pedicure, massage, or just join her for coffee. But you turn her down. Your daughter has dance, your son has drum lessons, and the laundry is calling your name. If you aren't there for them, there's no way they'll get their homework done or get to bed on time. So, you decline, saying, "Thanks for thinking of me, but I'll have to take a raincheck."

There are a thousand and one different scenarios that come to mind, each with a different variation of the ways we pull ourselves further away from our needs and dreams and justify it because we've positioned ourselves at the bottom of the totem pole.

And that's not fair to us ... or to the people we love.

Common Myths to Dispel:

- There's not enough time in the day.
- There should be two of me.
- I'd really like to (join the gym, take up painting, have a spa day, etc.), but it's not fair to my family. They need me too much.
- It's my job to be here for my family. I'll get around to what I want when they don't need me so much.
- Mom and Dad have been there for me my whole life. I owe it to them to put my life on hold now that they need me.

You get the picture. In every one of those myths, we put ourselves last and find a way to justify it. But we forget that when we give ourselves permission to put ourselves first, we give ourselves the care, the fuel, and the energy to be a better version of ourselves for those we love.

Reframing our thinking might seem difficult, especially if it stems from our childhood, but it is possible. All it takes is a shift in our thoughts.

Flip the switch, if you will. Swap that thought.

- A night out with my best friend is just what I need! The kids will be fine, and their mom will be happy.
- I owe it to my family to be happy and healthy. A little relaxation will reduce my stress, and I'll be calmer when I'm with them.
- I really want my kids to grow up and make their dreams come true. The best way to inspire them is to be a good example.
- I am worthy of my own time.

- I love myself enough to take care of myself before I take care of others.
- I cannot help anyone else if I let myself go.
- I get to take care of myself, or my family won't have anyone to take care of them.

Changing your thoughts will bring you a new perspective. The more you affirm those thoughts, the more they will influence your beliefs. Before long, you'll find that you're convinced that what is good for you is also good for those you love.

And when they see the happier, healthier, more attentive you, they'll agree. Then when things go wrong, and they sometimes will, they'll be the ones to remind you not to forget to put your oxygen mask on first, because they love and need you.

Self-love isn't selfish at all; it's selfless. It's not a luxury or a bonus; it's a necessity. Do it for you—do it for the people you love.

One Thought Away

SELF-CARE IS NOT A LUXURY

Changing your thoughts will bring you a new perspective. The more you affirm those thoughts, the more they will influence your beliefs. Before long, you'll understand that what is good for you, is also good for those you love.

Self-care isn't selfish; it's selfless. It's not a luxury or a bonus; it's a necessity. Do it for you—do it for the people you love.

1) What gaps do you have with your self-care?

2) What do you want your self-care to look like?

3) What is your plan to turn it around and by when?

#onethoughtaway | support@kerrytepedino.com | www.onethoughtawaybook.com

Conclusion

My hope is that this book has been able to support you in seeing your life and future in a different way--that you have had a new or deeper understanding that you absolutely can create anything in your life, with the right strategies and support around you.

I am a huge believer that anything is possible; the key is to stay in consistent action with what you learned in this book. Success doesn't happen as a one and done. It takes consistent attention and focus to create a desired result.

Your life is worth it.

You are worth it.

If you feel overwhelmed and don't know where to start, start small with where you are at. A one percent shift daily adds up to a big shift over time! You can do one percent today.

Your next steps are to print the chapter Printables out and hang them up where you see them often. Permeate your environment with the One Thought Away lessons all the time, everywhere. Be working with your brain on an unconscious level, so your brain can be working FOR you, even when you sleep.

If you are a woman over 21 years old and ready to transform, apply to be in one of our women's group coaching programs. This is where you not only will meet lifelong friends, but you'll see next-level transformation happen in your life in a very short period of time.

And, of course, I would love to discuss speaking opportunities in person or online if you feel that I can contribute value to your community.

And last, but not least, connect with me on Facebook, Instagram, and Linked In so we can stay connected and possibly work deeper together.

Tons of love,
Kerry xx

Resources

Please take advantage of the online resources we have created to support you in your transformation.

Visit www.OneThoughtAwayBook.com.

Join the One Thought Away Community in our private Facebook group, where you can interact with others and find support and encouragement. (www.facebook.com/groups/onethoughtawayproject)

Listen to visualizations and access the printables in this book by visiting www.OneThoughtAwayBook.com/Bonus

I look forward to helping you on the journey to your dream life!

About Kerry Tepedino

Kerry Tepedino, HHP, CCN, CST, is an internationally recognized Mindset Expert and the Founder/CEO of the One Thought Away Project. She is supporting thousands of women to overcome their limiting beliefs, so they can live the lives of their dreams. Join us and be delightfully surprised at how quickly you will see results.

Learn more at www.onethoughtawayproject.com